PERENNIALS

Antique Flowers

PERENNIALS

Enduring Classics for the Contemporary Garden

ROB PROCTOR

PHOTOGRAPHY BY ROB GRAY

WATERCOLOURS AND SUPPLEMENTAL
PHOTOGRAPHS BY THE AUTHOR

FOREWORD BY ROSEMARY VEREY

CASSELL

FOR DAVID

**We'll build our house
And chop our wood
And make our garden grow.**

Lyrics by Richard Wilbur

in CANDIDE

Cassell Publishers Limited
Villiers House
41/47 Strand
London
WC2N 5JE

First published in Great Britain 1990

A RUNNING HEADS BOOK

PERENNIALS was conceived and produced by
Running Heads Incorporated
55 West 21st Street
New York, NY 10010

A CIP record for this book is
available from the British Library

ISBN 0 304 34019 7

Typeset by Trufont Typographers, Inc.
Color separations by Hong Kong Scanner Craft Company, Ltd.
Printed and bound in Singapore by Times Offset Pte Ltd.

ACKNOWLEDGMENTS

There is a simple and beautiful garden in a village in East Anglia. The sign on the gate reads, "All who love flowers are welcome here." Without the generosity of gardeners like these, who opened their doors and shared their creations, this book would not have been possible. The photographs by Rob Gray capture the diverse characters of gardens, great and small, on two continents. I am grateful to the designers who arranged flowers for us, especially Robin Preston and Angela Overy.

To the gracious people who opened their gardens and homes to us, many thanks:

Richard Brittain
Diane Dalton
Beth Chatto
Diana Monday
Monica and Jeremy Pemberton
Lewis Hart
Rosemary Verey
Margaret Fuller
Mary and Procter Naylor
Christopher Lloyd
Bea Taplin
Anne Weckbaugh
Tweet Kimball
Peter Harley
Tom Peace
Karen and Jim Esquibel
Mary Kay Long and Dennis Unites
Nancy Stimson Watters
Elfreda Sacarto
Pat Thorpe
Don Hewitt and Marilyn Berger

Allen Haskell
Peter Stephens
Chris Lennon
Rennie Reynolds
The Cloisters
Denver Botanic Gardens
Nymans Garden
Sissinghurst Castle Garden
Kiftsgate Court Gardens
Owl House Gardens
Dowcra's Manor
Penshurst Place
Hever Castle
Hidcote Manor Garden
Scotney Castle Garden
Kew Royal Botanic Gardens
Cambridge University Botanic Garden
Old Sturbridge Village
Sundial Herb Garden
Graymoor Antiques

Special thanks to:
Deane Hall
Panayoti Kelaidis
Ray Daugherty
Lauren Springer
Rita Buchanan
Solange Gignac of The Helen Fowler
    Library, Denver Botanic Gardens
Pat Pachuta
Alcinda Cundiff
Nancy Ballek MacKinnon,
    Ballek's Garden Center
Jeanne Ruggles
Starr Tapp
Thornton's Antiques
Susan Sheridan
Lin Hulbert
Ian Beyer
Edward Connors
Annie Duncan
Andrew Pierce

C O N T E N T S

FOREWORD BY ROSEMARY VEREY

THERE ARE THREE ASPECTS OF perennials I particularly enjoy: they are reliable, coming up in the garden year after year, to be greeted as old friends; they increase in beauty and are easily multiplied for your own use and as presents for your gardening neighbours; and many of them have a fascinating history, stretching back several centuries. These aspects are generously explored by Rob Proctor in an affectionate, knowledgeable, and wide-ranging account that is, as he says, not about the history of perennials but rather about perennials with a history.

I know of no garden, however specialist, where perennials do not play a role, usually a key role. They are the stayers, the survivors. The may grow old in the garden's service and have to be replaced by a younger generation, but if they have proved their worth in the border their descendent will follow them.

Flowers—like clothes—go in and out of fashion. Some are cherished, others improved, still others lost. Rob Proctor's selection of antique perennials includes our favourite flowers—campanulas and clematis, iris, lilium and geranium. So, as with all old friends, it is interesting to learn their history and trace their antecedents: their birthplace, the plant hunters who sought them out, the authors who popularized them, the nurseries who sold them, their old names and new varieties. There is a thrill in discovering that the Rapunzel of the fairy tale was named after *Campanula rapunculus*, or that a plant you have and love in your own garden was first grown by John Tradescant for Charles II.

While the old gardeners haunt our every border, there is a feeling of adventure of hybridizing or discovering a new variety. I was visited recently by a young German girl; her great-grandfather was Georg Arends, who started his nursery in 1888 and is immortalized by so many enduring plants hybridized by him—*Astilbe × arendsii* and *Aconitum arendsii* are just two of them. In our own time Margery Fish, the great champion of cottage gardens, and Valerie Finnis of alpine plant fame have given their names to plants known on both sides of the Atlantic. And there is a perennial, *Lavatera thuringiaca* 'Barnsley', with which I am particularly proud to be associated. I cannot claim pride of primogeniture, only that of stumbling on its beauty and then propagating it for other gardeners to enjoy.

The feeling of adventure extends beyond the discovery and naming of new perennials. Since the turn of the century a trend has developed in American gardening which has taken an exciting turn away from the mainstream of European gardening, becoming stylized in a bold, imaginative, thoroughly modern way. In this development perennials—old and new—have played an important part. Wherever I go in America these days, talk of perennials is in the air, and American visitors to my garden in Gloucestershire are full of questions about the perennials we grow. Often I can tell them that a particular plant they admire is a native of their own country. Will it suit their particular soil and compete successfully with their harsh or hot climate, they enquire.

The traditional *entente cordiale* between our two countries is as strong a thread as ever. In 1980, when Peggy and David Rockefeller were in England, they were investigating the scope of perennials to grow in their famous garden in Maine. And last year I had the privilege of meeting Lady Bird Johnson and discussing the wonderful work she has promoted in the planting of annual and perennial wildflowers along the highways of her native Texas.

Inspiration comes from knowledge, observation and experiment. However large or small your garden, this book will lead you forward.

Abutilon and *schizanthus* grow in the conservatory at Barnsley House, OPPOSITE. The striped form of *Geranium pratense*, LEFT, is known as Queen Anne's Needlework. *Campanula poscharskyana* covers a stone wall, BELOW.

I'VE ALWAYS LOVED FLOWERS. I'm told that as a baby, when turned loose on the lawn I would head to the flower beds and eat petunias. Perhaps we saw things from a different perspective as children, but I'm almost positive that the bumblebees visiting the weeping branches of our Bridal Veil were inordinately large when I was five. The corn in the garden where I buried the entire population of my sister's dolls house (a crime I never confessed) surely grew taller than those in my present garden. The hemlock growing round our chicken coops was a dense jungle, and a feeling of danger still pervades that memory. Wildflowers decorated the "natural" settings I created in shoe boxes for captive horned toads. The few days the toads spent in the paradise of rocks and sand, complete with jar-lid pond, must have spoiled them for life after I returned them to the wild.

The real turning point in my young life came when I was eight, and we moved to town. I have only a dim recollection of our house. What was important was the garden of the house across the street—we faced a horticultural Disneyland. Nothing before or since has seemed so wonderful. Flanking the drive were junipers trimmed into topiary baskets with handles, brimming with geraniums. Rambling roses and clematis sprawled over the porch. There were deep borders and a star-shaped rose bed. The gardener, Katie, did not have children and was unofficial grandmother to all of us in the neighbourhood. I was the most persistent child of the lot, earning the title of her shadow. I wanted to learn all there was to know about flowers, and Katie was a patient teacher. I learned to

AUTHOR'S PREFACE

Ornamental onions—*Allium senescens, A. tuberosum,* and *Tulbaghia violacea*—have survived over the years, ABOVE. *Meconopsis cambrica* hovers above *Geranium himalayense,* OPPOSITE.

remove the spent blossoms of pansies—a task known as deadheading. Her pansies were self-sown, or as Katie put it, "They come up volunteer." I learned about planting, staking, dividing, transplanting, weeding, and much more. My mother never had to worry about my whereabouts, and I highly resented the interruptions for swimming lessons. I had little aptitude—I can barely manage the semblance of a breaststroke to this day. But what I learned from Katie stuck. In a what-I-want-to-be-when-I-grow-up paper written in school, I stated that I intended to be an artist and grow flowers. This was met with both amusement and horror from practical parents who could see no future in either. We moved again in two years, but my fate was sealed. My sister

and I fashioned rock gardens whenever we had accumulated enough stones from family trips to the mountains. (I still recall our rockeries, planted mainly with sedums and hens-and-chicks. We thought them absolutely splendid, although I suspect their dog's-grave shapes may have suggested a rash of pet deaths.)

Houseplants and window boxes had to sustain my horticultural urges during years of college and apartment living. When at last I had my own garden, I planted the flowers I had loved at Katie's. Pansies, poppies, and primroses thrive for me as they did for her. Sweet William, alyssum, and Flowering Tobacco scent the air. Lamb's Ears and Lady's Mantle skirt borders of veronica, lilies, and meadow rue. These were the plants I knew and cherished. Gardening fashion has never played a conscious part in my garden, and I have begun to realize that these are not just the flowers of my childhood memories, but also those of our ancestors. They forge living links between many generations. A gardener, perhaps more than anyone else, is aware of the change of seasons and the passage of time. While time may pass most pleasantly in a garden, we know that each of us will have the chance to make only a certain number of gardens. I count each year as another garden, and each autumn wistfully acknowledge that another will be gone soon. Gardening is a daily, yearly, and lifelong practice. It's a strange combination of science and art, specific to each gardener. (There are gardens where neither is applied, but I liked to think these are the exceptions.) Good horticulture is simply a matter of learning a few basic skills—like digging a hole or planting a seed—but art is something else entirely, although art and gardening are inexorably intertwined. Experimentation is the mother of excellence.

Fashion plays a part in our gardens whether we want to admit it or not. Fashion may be positive, resurrecting a good plant from obscurity; or it may be negative, banishing an equally good plant sometimes, sadly, to the point of extinction. A rage for a new species has occasionally spelled death for an old one. I don't think the world really needs another dinner-plate dahlia, but I'm happy they are here for whoever would want them, as long as astrantias are also available for whoever has the taste to grow them.

In comparing modern with antique flowers, we may discover that bigger and brighter are not always better, and the word "charm" is much undervalued. While I will defend any gardener's right to grow a flower with the size and colour of a day-glow Frisbee®, I certainly question the reason. If masses of floral colour are all that is required in a garden, we might as well opt for plastic imitations. We would not have to fuss with all that messy planting and tiresome watering. Some might argue that those who do not see well may enjoy the bright blobs of modern monstrosities, but Gertrude Jekyll, whose vision was poor even as a young woman, created gardens of unequalled colour subtlety early in this century. Gardens are, happily, much more than pop art canvases. Many of us are rediscovering the art of growing almost-lost flowers. We can be free of modern affectations. We can ignore the current vogue of "installing plant material." (That phrase is abominable,

presuming as little passion as plumbing.) "Planting," a word that has served well for centuries, is a noble and, yes, sometimes a passionate endeavour.

This is a book, not about the history of

perennial flowers, but rather about perennials with a history. Romans, medieval monks, Victorian plant hunters, and our own grandmothers have inspired chapters. Each of us may add to the stories.

INTRODUCTION

THE STORY OF
ANTIQUE
PERENNIALS

"NOSTALGIA FOR THE PAST HAS brought with it a revival of taste for the old-fashioned flowers; the flaked pinks and carnations, the double primroses, the broken tulips, the double Sweet Williams. Perhaps it is not only nostalgia for an age which, rightly or wrongly, we esteem to have been happier than our own, as it was certainly more leisurely, but also a natural reaction against the exaggerated blooms we are offered today; size not subtlety." From *In Your Garden Again*, Vita Sackville-West.

The flowers growing in our gardens have histories stretching back to before we brought them home from the nursery. Some were created only yesterday by breeders, others can be traced through time to the ancients. Much of the pleasure of growing them is derived from learning their histories. The perennials featured within these pages have all been growing in gardens since before the beginning of the twentieth century. Their designation as antique reflects at least a hundred years of cultivation, although many are much, much older. When a date of introduction is given, it refers to the time when a plant was first grown in England, where—more than anywhere else—a standard of horticulture developed that has been felt throughout the world.

The American gardening tradition is largely an English one. Early colonists brought both the plants and the sensibilities of their homeland, and the ties have continued and strengthened. Though many other European cultures have a prominent role in the development of the English and American garden, these are still Western influences. Other cultures

have had strong horticultural traditions, but in many cases, such as the Aztecs, their knowledge died with the destruction of their civilization. There is little interest in re-creating an authentic Aztec garden at present, so the focus here is on the flowers grown in Europe and North America.

As long as flowers have been grown, they have been picked and brought inside. The symbolism of flowers pervaded every culture, from Egypt to the Orient. Greeks and Romans fashioned wreaths and garlands. One of the first depictions of a flower arrangement is on a Roman mosaic, from the first century of this era, where a simple woven basket holds a few roses, pinks, and anemones. Aromatic plants like lavender and Sweet Woodruff sweetened the air of musty medieval rooms. Monks decorated altars on saints' days, and posies were laid on graves. Colonial ladies picked handfuls of marigolds and scented geraniums to take to church; sniffing the pungent bouquets gave them a wide-awake look during lengthy sermons. Master European painters like Jan Brueghel portrayed glorious bouquets unequalled before or since. The Victorians popularized corsages, and brought the art of arranging to new heights of extravagance. Schools, cults, and trends have proliferated. To some, arranging flowers is a discipline. Katherine S. White was a lady who loved flowers and bouquets, but none of the artificial regulations imposed by society. In *Onward and Upward in the Garden*, she rails against pretence: "I like it better when Americans are simply themselves . . . bringing in a few flowers to brighten the house and arranging them, considering no inheritance or style, following no rules, imitating no

other civilization, and using the nearest container that comes in handy, whether it be an old beanpot or pickle jar, an expensive Steuben or Finnish crystal vase, a piece of antique china or a modern ceramic."

She tells the tale of a local flower show, where a friend had used Baby's Breath in an arrangement. She relates how, ". . . a visiting judge had written this note to her: 'You really should *not* use Baby's Breath. It would never be accepted in a standard show.' (There is, by the way, no rule in the 'Handbook' that says this.) Now, I'm not wild about Baby's Breath; I remember from the early part of the century too many florists' bouquets of roses that were ruined by being stuffed with it. But it occurred to me that if Odilon Redon could paint this delicate flower into some of his still lifes of flowers there was no reason at all that a Maine woman should be admonished for including it in her arrangements if it was her pleasure to do so." This is a perfect example of fashion dictating what is to be grown. The fortunes of Baby's Breath, *Gypsophila paniculata*, have waned from over-use or poor use. It is ironic that the look-alike Sea Kale, *Crambe maritima*, languished in obscurity for most of this century and has only recently achieved recognition in the finest gardens.

Rules aside, flower arranging has been subject to the same dictates and whims as the garden, but some flowers have remained favourites in every age, while others have fallen from grace. (The humble bouquets in this book follow no rules and pretend to be nothing more than pretty flowers picked for pleasure, and to further

show particular blossoms more closely and in association with others. We had great fun, my friends and I, plundering our gardens with abandon.)

Perennial plants play important parts in most gardens, although defining "perennial" is tricky. In the broadest interpretation, a perennial is a plant that lives for three or more years, which separates it from annuals, which survive only one growing season, and biennials, which grow one year and flower and die the next. What sets perennials apart from annuals and to a lesser extent, biennials, is the durability of their roots and the ability to survive winter cold. What is perennial in any garden is determined by climate—what is perennial in Dallas will not necessarily be perennial in Dundee. The reverse is also true.

Herbaceous perennials—non-woody plants that die to the ground each winter—are generally what gardeners mean when they speak of perennials, but some bulbs, vines, and sub-shrubs may also be regarded as perennials. The distinction is up to the individual gardener. One tongue-in-cheek but oh-so-true definition of perennial, which I particularly like, is offered by Henry Beard and Roy McKie in *Gardening: A Gardener's Dictionary.* It reads, "Perennial: Any plant which, had it lived, would have bloomed year after year."

A word should be said about the distinction between species and cultivated varieties. A species is a nonimproved specific type developed by nature. A "cultivar" is a selection, found by a sharp-eyed plantsman, which displays a slightly different trait than the species, such as being taller, shorter, or producing more

Baby's Breath, *Gypsophila paniculata,* has suffered from over-use by arrangers in the past. In a loosely-structured bouquet, ABOVE, its airy white sprays set a backdrop for the lavender flowers of scabiosa, Dusty Miller, and the leaves of bergenia. BELOW, a perennial that is similar, albeit larger, than Baby's Breath, *Crambe cordifolia,* known as the Giant Sea Kale, receives a prominent position in a garden tapestry of silver foliage and white flowers.

flowers or flowers of a different colour. White forms of many flowers occur naturally, and are often highly valued by gardeners. A hybrid is the offspring between two (or more) different species, and usually shares characteristics from the parents. When dealing with antique plants, the lines between cultivars and hybrids are blurred, since their origin is often unknown. To complicate matters, hybrids often occur naturally, as many gardeners can attest. The Victorians labelled such flowers, rather disapprovingly, as "promiscuous." Some species are highly variable, and wild populations can display a diversity of forms and habits.

Some antique plants are common ones that have gone in and out of fashion but have never left the care of gardeners who didn't put much stock in fashion. Others have never been extremely popular, for various reasons. We depend, to a large extent, on the nursery trade to make and keep plants available. Why some plants catch the public's fancy, and others don't, is anyone's guess. Ease of propagation is an important factor: plants with exacting requirements need more labour and are more expensive to produce. Demand is usually the bottom line, but the public can't demand what it doesn't know. Some unusual plants have been cherished by plantsmen and keen gardeners who grew them without fanfare. And since gardens have been so strongly influenced by English garden writers for such a long time, plants that don't thrive in an English climate are not likely to have received much favourable press. It's an old game on both sides of the Atlantic: we covet what we cannot cultivate. I can't count my

many (failed) experiments growing species that need abundant moisture and humidity. They may thrive in Oregon, in Kent, or even in Massachusetts, but die with me. Conversely, the sun-lovers, the flowers that

A white hybrid seedling of Everblooming Bleeding-heart, *Dicentra eximia*, ABOVE, appeared in a shady bed in Beth Chatto's garden. BELOW, the white flowers of Gas Plant, *Dictamnus albus*, are prized. The blue flowers of Jacob's Ladder, *Polemonium foliosissimum*, are a feature of gardens in late spring, combined with *Primula sikkimensis*, OPPOSITE.

need real heat to come to perfection, are likely to flop or rot in "more favourable" climes. They might be a big hit in Kansas City or Atlanta, but it's unlikely that English writers like Gertrude Jekyll or

William Robinson would have had any praise for them. Happily, there are a great many flowers of such a hardy constitution and accommodating nature (like the gardeners who tend them) that they will thrive for nearly every gardener on either shore. Certainly the degree of perfection to which they can be grown varies, but peonies, poppies, and polemoniums grace gardens great and small in the most diverse areas. Clever and lucky gardeners who take scant notice of hardiness ratings have found some so-called tender plants that do well for them. Plants can't read hardiness charts, and the limits for many plants are still being tested.

There are always failures. I have a friend, a famous gardener, whose opinion is valued and who is always being asked for advice on sickly and dying plants. His philosophy is that deaths in the garden are not very important—if you're not killing off plants, he says, you're not trying very hard. To be afraid to try is much worse than to try and fail. Stagnation is the great enemy of gardens, not plants that die. Great gardeners are made, not born, and the grit of their determination comes from the failures, as well as the successes.

Beautiful gardens have been carved from the most inhospitable places. Flowers travel with gardeners to new homes, across a town or across an ocean, where they must adapt or perish. French Huguenots, fleeing to England to escape religious persecution, brought with them beloved primroses, roses, and pinks. Colonists faced the New World with seeds and sprigs of herbs and cherished plants. Lilacs, iris, and the fern-leaf peony traversed the American Great Plains with settlers, facing

rigorous conditions. They survived, and these plant "pioneers" have mingled with the native flora to create new gardening styles. Throughout the centuries gardeners have struggled to combine the old and new. There's hardly a place where it's easy to garden, and the gardens we make are always in danger of being reclaimed by nature. As Henry Mitchell says, "There are no green thumbs or black thumbs. There are only gardeners and non-gardeners.

Traditional flowers of cottage gardens, Oriental Poppies and Honeysuckle, are viewed through a doorway, ABOVE. OPPOSITE, the visions of one man, George Russell, resulted in a spectrum of colourful *Lupinus polyphyllus* hybrids.

Gardeners are the ones who ruin after ruin get on with the high defiance of nature herself, creating, in the very face of her chaos and tornado, the bower of roses and the pride of irises. It sounds very well to garden a 'natural way.' You may see the natural way in any desert, swamp, any leech-filled laurel hell. Defiance, on the other hand, is what makes gardeners."

Tenacity and persistence are traits

shared by gardeners through time. Wild-flowers have been tamed, and cultivated flowers have been improved. Explorers have risked their lives to bring home exotic species. Hybridists have spent life-times in pursuit of their dreams. One such man, George Russell, who lived near Wolverhampton, dreamed of improving the common Blue Lupin. Over the course of more than twenty-five years, he crossed and re-crossed seedlings. Even when of-fered exorbitant sums by nurserymen to sell the plants, he refused; he had not yet reached his goal. When at last he was satisfied, the world was stunned—the lupin had been transformed. Its colours, now as brilliant and varied as a paint-box, are a tribute to one gardener's de-termination.

Gardening has become the more chal-lenging as our choices disappear. The plants from the past, those that have survived adversity in countless gardens, threaten to disappear through neglect. Some species are extinct in the wild, and countless man-made hybrids have vanished over the past several centuries. It is already impossible to replicate any of Miss Jekyll's gardens as she planned them, because many of her favourites are gone. Progress marches on, even in gardening. Much of the world has been explored, and though there are still species to be discovered that will find their way into gardens, the golden days of the plant hunters are past. We will never again see days like those of the eighteenth and nineteenth centuries, when the flood of plants from around the world filled English and American gardens with exotic flora. The new frontier is the past.

CHAPTER ONE

THE WRITTEN
HISTORY
OF FLOWERS

PLANTS HAVE BEEN CULTIVATED since the beginning of civilization. Food crops have always been of the foremost importance. We don't know when the first flower was grown for pleasure, strictly for its beauty alone. It is evident that in nearly every culture, as soon as it rose above the subsistence level, flowers began to be intertwined into the arts of the society, from pottery and textiles to architecture and murals. The Babylonians were famous for their gardening skills. Egyptian columns display stylized lotus blossoms, and it may have been a queen of the Nile, Hatshepsut, who inaugurated a long tradition of plant-hunting expeditions. About 1600 B.C., she sent workers into Africa, seeking plants to decorate a new temple. Their greatest find was a tree that yielded an aromatic resin called frankincense.

The horticultural knowledge of the Golden Age of Greece is preserved in the works of Theophrastus, who conducted the famous school of philosophy founded by Aristotle, and in *De Materia Medica* by the physician Dioscorides, which was the primary botanical source until well into the seventeenth century. Much of what we know about early horticulture is preserved in the writings of Gaius Plinius Secundus, otherwise known as Pliny the Elder. In his *Natural History*, this ambitious Roman nobleman compiled and summarized the works of over a hundred previous writers on the subjects of plants, animals, minerals, and the like. It provides our greatest insight into these matters during the classical age, since most of his sources have vanished. A victim of his own scientific curiosity, Pliny perished while viewing the eruption of Mount Vesuvius in A.D. 79.

The next sources of horticultural import were not to appear until medieval times, in the form of the herbals. Based fuzzily on the classical texts, combined with superstition, the herbals were produced to compile knowledge about the useful plants. Healing (and learning) were largely the province of monks, who copied much of the herbal knowledge of the day in manuscripts. They believed that God had provided curing plants for every ill, if only man could discover the special power of each plant. Surely He would have provided clues; a plant's appearance, especially a resemblance to a part of the body, would indicate how it could be used. A signature—the outward sign of a herb's inner virtue—gradually was accepted. The Doctrine of Signatures may seem farfetched today, but it flourished in the Middle Ages. There is a certain logic to some of the beliefs. The appearance of the walnut, with its hard "skull" and brainlike interior, was an obvious signature, indicating its use to treat head injuries and mental problems. It was pronounced that Hound's Tongue, *Cynoglossum officinale*, so named for its rough leaves, was a remedy for "mad doggebit." Plants with yellow sap, such as Greater Celandine, *Chelidonium majus*, or Horned Poppy, *Glaucium flavum*, could be employed to treat jaundice. The recurving flower stem of the forget-me-not indicated its use to treat scorpion stings; this may have been comforting but was rarely put to the test in Britain. The perforated leaves of St. John's Wort clearly indicated its ability to heal skin wounds. Many of the plants were employed for a number of ailments; garlic was said to cure well over fifty complaints.

The yellow sap of Horned Poppy, *Glaucium flavum* 'Corniculatum', ABOVE, was formerly thought to be an effective remedy for jaundice under the Doctrine of Signatures, which sought to find an outward sign for a plant's inner virtue.

Death was disastrous; in less than twenty years three-quarters of the population of the two continents died. Three centuries later, the Great Plague of London wreaked further havoc.

When Henry VIII quarrelled with the Pope over his marriage to Anne Boleyn, a new gardening era began. With the dissolution of the monasteries, about 1530, a thousand years of horticultural information was lost to a single generation. The ultimate effect was to advance the practice of gardening—by necessity. The common people were forced to grow for themselves the herbs they had relied on the monks to provide. The cottage garden had its humble beginnings, as villagers began to grow comfrey, wormwood, sage, borage, and horehound to treat themselves. The gardens of the disbanded monasteries yielded *Lilium candidum*, the Madonna Lily, used then as a medicinal plant but likewise admired for its beauty and scent. Culinary herbs were added to the new gardens, mostly to disguise bad or salted meats. Aromatic herbs like bedstraw and lavender were grown for strewing in foul-smelling rooms. The laity replaced clerics as the caretakers of the healing knowledge. Gardens remained largely utilitarian; life was too harsh, and the times too unsettled, to permit gardening for pleasure alone.

John Gerard was a barber and surgeon from London with a passion for plants. *The Herball or Generall Historie of Plants*, published in 1597, is the most famous of the English herbals. Gerard is the most quoted writer of his age, although it is likely most of the work attributed to him belongs rightly to an unsung Flemish botanist, Rembert Dodoens. A publisher had hired

Medicine was still in the dark ages, so to speak, and a great deal of the cures of the day were more wishful thinking than anything else. It is small wonder that superstition played such a large part in healing. Minor ailments could be treated with some effect, but against serious illness there was little defence. In 1339, an epidemic began in Constantinople and swept through Europe and Asia. The Black

Dr. Priest (whose first name has vanished) to translate Dodoens' work into English, but the doctor died before the project was finished. Gerard came into possession of the manuscript, completed the translation, did some rearranging, and published it under his own name. The woodcuts for the text, some 1,800 of them, were bought by the publisher from a herbal printed six years earlier, which in turn had secured them from various sources. Gerard's skills as a botanist were not sufficient to match all the illustrations with the correct names,

Comfrey, *Symphytum officinale,* ABOVE, was one of the herbs grown in English monastery gardens and its healing properties earned it the common name Knit-bone.

and he called on Matthias de L'Obel, who was later commemorated by the genus *Lobelia,* to assist him. Even so, errors remained until a second edition in 1633. Despite the disreputable circumstances under which it was created, *The Herball* provides a wealth of information, the style is highly readable and entertaining, and it carried great weight at the time.

It is interesting to compare it with the *New Herbal,* written entirely—so far as we know—by William Turner and published thirty years earlier. Turner was a physician and supporter of the Reformation whose strong opinions often put him at odds with the crown; he was a fugitive abroad during the reigns of Henry VIII and Mary. His interest was strictly medical, whereas Gerard was interested in all plants real or imagined. (He claimed to have seen the fabled Barnacle Tree, from the fruit of which sea fowl were said to hatch.)

Thirty years after Gerard's herbal, John Parkinson's *Paradisi in Sole, Paradisus Terrestris* (the title was a little pun in Latin—Park-in-sun—on his own name) was the first English book devoted solely to ornamental plants. Parkinson was trained as an apothecary, but found himself totally caught up in the beauty of flowers, and it is of a "Garden of Pleasant Flowers" that he wrote. Parkinson's own journey of discovery mirrored the transformation of the garden. Peace and prosperity had arrived, and the English flower garden was born.

Just as the true sciences of botany and medicine began their modern evolution, along came a figure described as having "a bonnet as full of bees as a border of catmint on a bright sunny morning." The old Doctrine of Signatures was given considerable credence in the mid-1600s by Nicholas Culpeper, an unorthodox doctor who angered the medical establishment by translating the *Pharmacopaeia* from Latin into English for the masses to read, breaking the doctors' monopoly. He mixed astrology into medicinal theories: he assigned every plant and disease to the influence of a planet. By treating an illness

with an herb governed by the same sign, or, conveniently, by an opposite, Culpeper invoked the wrath of the College of Physicians. He claimed that he alone acted by reason, and could prove all his theories through his astrological findings. Since he had made everything up in the first place, it was pretty hard for the medical establishment, which he branded as "proud, insulting, and domineering dunces," to argue with him. This new breed of scientists questioned the whole premise of the doctrine. They were disturbed that some useful plants had no apparent signatures, and worse, many of the "cures" had little effect. One of the first of the true English botanists, John Ray, born just eleven years after Culpeper, wrote near the end of the seventeenth century, "All that I find mentioned and collected by authors, seem to me rather fancied by men, than designed by nature." Ray was the author of a landmark work on botany, *Methodus Plantarum Nova,* in 1682. Of the lives and works of the two contemporaries, Culpeper and Ray, it is interesting to note that Ray lived to be seventy-seven, and his contributions are largely forgotten; Culpeper died at thirty-eight from consumption, yet his herbal ran through edition after edition, and herbal medicine books of today still quote and revere his writings.

The Doctrine of Signatures (as distinct from folk medicine, which employed many plants later found to have valuable active properties) failed to produce any breakthroughs, with one accidental exception. Assuming that marsh-growing willows thrived where rheumatism was prevalent, a doctor began to treat his patients with a willow bark decoction. He had discovered salicylic acid, which centuries later was synthesized and sold as aspirin.

American writers chronicled the journey of plants to the New World, and the many new and wondrous species discovered on virgin shores. John Bartram, in whose footsteps his son William followed, was called "the greatest natural botanist in the world" by Linnaeus. By horseback, canoe, and on foot, he travelled from Canada to Florida, and deep into the Ohio Valley. His garden near Philadelphia was the nation's first botanical garden. His ambitious papers and diaries provide a wealth of information on the state of gardening and everything else in the mid-1700s. John Clayton was an English naturalist who came to Virginia and served as clerk of Gloucester County for fifty-one years; during that time he developed the finest garden in the country, and became a close friend of Bartram's. His *Flora Virginica* was published in 1762. The native Spring Beauty, *Claytonia virginica*, bears his name.

Both men corresponded with Peter Collinson, an English Quaker wool merchant and friend of Benjamin Franklin, whom he advised in the electricity experiments. Collinson sent European plants to his friends, and arranged for American plants to be sent to England. The letters between Collinson and another American naturalist, John Custis of Williamsburg, depict the joys and frustrations of sending plants across the ocean.

George Washington, who married the widow of Custis's son, devoted himself to his agricultural pursuits and the beautification of Mount Vernon, time permitting. His diaries carefully detail the plants he

grew. Even more meticulous in his record keeping, Thomas Jefferson excelled at many things, gardening among them. *Notes on the State of Virginia* and his *Garden Book* provide an accurate picture of the flowers of colonial days. His famous quotation, "But though an old man, I am but a young gardener," is a telling one from the brilliant statesman and scientist. *The Flower Garden*, by Joseph Breck, chronicles the state of American horticulture midway through the nineteenth century. Peter Henderson's works, published a mere forty years later, document the amazing strides made, and the wealth of plants known and grown during the late Victorian period.

Botany as a science took giant strides forward with Linnaeus. He was born Carl von Linné in 1707 in Sweden, the son of a parson. After he was internationally recognized as a naturalist, he adopted the Latinized form Linnaeus, as was the fashion of the day. His *Species Plantarum*, published in 1753, gave botany a system of classification, and a language. Pre-Linnaean terminology was difficult to understand, and by grouping related plants into one genus, and giving particular ones exact names, called specific ephitets, he simplified a nightmarish labyrinth of nomenclature. Linnaeus was just thirty when he perfected his system, and he swept away the remnants of the superstitious "science" of the Middle Ages, which he deemed "a mere chaos of confusion, whose mother was barbarity, whose father dogmatism, and whose nurse prejudice." There were holdouts against his system, and some conservatives were wary of the upstart who would "confound" their work.

Linnaeus's search for the truth during

his travels made him enemies, as in Germany, where the city of Hamburg was the proud home of the Seven-headed Hydra, supposedly a Greek relic brought back by Crusaders. Upon examining the creature, which was a precursor of modern freak tourist attractions, Linnaeus discovered the hydra was actually a skillful fake—seven weasel heads attached to a body, all covered with snakeskin, complete with two bird-claw feet. This revelation was not greeted with the spirit in which it had been given, and Linnaeus left town.

Scarlet Bugler, *Penstemon barbatus*, ABOVE, was an early import to English gardens from the western territories of the United States, although it was initially assigned to the genus *Chelone*.

If not a hero in Hamburg, Linnaeus single-handedly revolutionized the study of natural science. Plantsmen owe him an enormous debt. I know some gardeners who cannot abide the Latin names, but common ones inevitably vary from county to county, nation to nation, and century to century. We should not lose them, but they are more poetry than science. When precision is important, the case is won by the botanists. The Latin names, aside from some tongue-twisting, are universally understood. Perhaps intimidating at first, they can be the occasion of a great deal of fun and satisfaction. For example, I derive a small pleasure from saying the rhythmic *Chrysanthemum leucanthemum*. I will be very much annoyed if they change that one, but as the progress of botany goes on, plants are reclassified and, to the dismay of gardeners, renamed. Here is where botanists and gardeners part company. Classification of plants is largely by the study of reproductive processes. Botanists sometimes find it necessary to assign some plants to a different genus or create an entirely new one. Even worse, in studying old papers, it is occasionally found that a species was discovered and named earlier than previously thought. Botanists, being courteous, defer to the first name, meaning that gardeners can never be entirely secure. *Hortus Third* has, in general, been used as the taxonomic reference on the scientific names of plants in this work. In a few cases, where opinions are deeply divided, it seems best to opt for the classifications most widely held by gardeners.

I like some of the old names. I'm sorry we traded in *Funkia* for *Hosta*, and *Tritoma* for *Kniphofia*. *Didiscus* will always mean the Blue Lace Flower to me; I will never warm up to *Trachymene*. On the other hand, I'm relieved we now say *Bergenia* instead of *Megasea*. And be thankful the name of *Czacksia* didn't stick for St. Bruno's Lily, which started out as *Anthericum*, and which for now is called *Paradisea*. Somewhere along the line, *Pentstemon* lost its first *t*, and

ABOVE, a wild flower of the American west, *Eschscholzia californica*, otherwise known as California Poppy, is called *Copa de Ora* (or cup of gold) in Spanish.

Eschscholzia sometimes gains one after the second *l*. Most gardeners, sensibly, stick with California Poppy, avoiding the controversy altogether.

We may think how easy the name game was for the cottage gardeners, who didn't give a hang about scientific nomenclature. They seemed to have a knack for finding the most lyrical words by which to call their favourite flowers. Every village worth

its salt was engaged in this practice, so it seems, and some are so charming in their vernacular as to totally obscure the origins. It can be assumed that the more folk names a plant has, the deeper its roots go into antiquity.

The pansy has more names than most. Shakespeare dubbed it Love-in-idleness, but he was not the only Englishman who could turn a phrase. Consider Three-faces-

under-a-hood, Herb Trinity, Jump-up-and-kiss-me, Lover's-thoughts, Heartsease, Kiss-me-at-the-garden-gate, Eyebright, and Cull-me-to-you. Most of these denote the flower as one of romance, although the last one gives me pause. Our current common name (just try one of the others at your local garden centre) is derived from the French *pensée*, merely meaning "thoughts." Shakespeare saw it both ways, and in a rare case of straightforwardness he said, "There is pansies, that's for thoughts."

Or take *Dianthus*. The name signifies it as Jove's flower, and harks back to the ancient Athenians. Gardeners today usually call the larger ones carnations. This name first was used by Turner in 1538 as *Incarnacyon*. Others called them Coronations, perhaps because the toothed petals resembled crowns, or because the blossoms were woven into garlands by the Greeks. The smaller ones we call pinks. This name was derived not from the colour of the flower, as might be surmised, but from the Dutch word *pink-oog*, meaning a twinkling eye. The colour name originated from this flower (rather than the other way around). At various times, an array of other names were bestowed: Sops-in-wine (it was used to flavour wine and ale), gilofrea, gerofleis, gillyvor, ielopher, jilliver, gelyfloure, clove-gilofre, gilloflower, feathered gillofer. Most writers had pretty much the same general idea, but by the time the spelling was standardized as *gillyflower*, the name was obsolete. To further confuse matters, stocks and wallflowers were both called gillyflowers.

Perceptive gardeners through the ages have selected particular individuals with special traits. Long before the process of

The "faces" of pansies have held a special fascination for gardeners for centuries. ABOVE, the diminutive *Viola cornuta* 'Jackanapes' is an old garden favourite. The fancy pansies, BELOW, properly *Viola × wittrockiana*, trace their ancestry to the tiny wild *Viola tricolor* of Great Britain. The florists of the eighteenth century improved them through selective breeding.

hybridization was known and understood, man attempted to nurture the occasional mutation that possessed a brighter colour, better scent, or different form. It didn't take long for him to try to influence it. Pliny the Elder, in the first century of this era, mistakenly advised that by soaking a bulb in red wine, one could change a white lily to purple. The study of genetics was almost two millennia away. Even its most famous proponent, Gregor Mendel, an Austrian monk who studied the peas he grew (and may have fudged his data to prove his theories), died forgotten in 1884, his work still unaccepted. In the meantime, selection in the garden continued, albeit haphazardly. It was understood that when the seeds of the best flowers were saved, the offspring often were as good or better. The first deliberate hybrid can't be determined, but selection has been going on since prehistoric times. (Heads of corn no bigger than a thumb have been discovered by archeologists in caves. Corn is not found growing wild anywhere in the world, and it is only through selection by various ancient peoples that the giant kernels were developed.)

The English, who had the time and the inclination, began in earnest about 1750 to change the faces of their flowers. This began the years of the florists—not as we know them today in flower shops, making bouquets and thrilling other people's lovers on Valentine's Day—but amateur growers who specialized in raising flowers for show. As is the case with keen enthusiasts in any hobby, strict guidelines and standards were soon set. The "ideal" for any flower is apt to be arbitrary and subject to the whims of fashion. The florists were as determined

as the current breeders of daylilies, iris, great Danes, or quarter horses.

Among the flowers that received the most attention were pinks, stocks, pansies, tulips, primroses, anemones, and hyacinths. The first recorded floral exhibition, of gold-laced polyanthus primroses, was in 1769. It ushered in the grand tradition of flower shows still found in every city, town, and county fair. Many of the best florists were weavers, city-dwellers with tiny garden plots where they coddled prize flowers; the laced pinks of the silk weavers of the town of Paisley were famous.

The number of varieties of the florists' flowers produced was staggering. Some, judging from the survivors, were incredibly beautiful, others truly bizarre. The tradition of the florists, who worked at home, flourished until the middle of nineteenth century. In the introduction to *Hardy Florists' Flowers* in 1879, the Rev. Francis Horner wrote, ". . . the hand-loom weaver worked behind his loom, able to watch his flowers (in their pots) as closely as his work, his labour and his pleasure intermingled, interwoven as intimately as his silken threads."

The history of the auricula primroses illustrates the era of the florists. Originally of modest Swiss Alpine descent, through careful breeding *Primula auricula* developed unusual colours such as olive-greens, dusky purples, and tortoiseshell shades, all with a characteristic mealy dusting called farina. Described in the late seventeenth century as "charming painted ladies that are all powdered," the show varieties could easily be spoiled by rain. Florists took increasing pains to protect them, resorting to growing them in pots, elaborately staged and

sheltered. Culture was to become very strange. A passage in *The Retir'd Gardener* warns, quite rightly, that we might be startled upon learning that the auricula "has a singular propensity for meat, and that a good part of its bloom is actually owing, like the alderman's, to this consumption of flesh. Juicy pieces of meat are placed about the root, so that it may in some measure be said to live on blood." The author obviously had an axe to grind with auricula florists, as well as with his city councillors. One particularly fanatical fancier (an alderman?) was well known for the batches of nasty and highly malodorous composts he devised for his plants. He purchased three geese to provide essential droppings. The geese broke loose one day, and to the satisfaction of his neighbours, proceeded to destroy his precious auricula collection.

Cities grew larger, the factories gradually absorbed the weavers, and consequently many of the old varieties were lost. Curiously, the upper class had never had much affection for the show flowers, especially the auriculas. The labour to grow them to perfection was too expensive even for the gentry, and the drab colours did not show to advantage in the open garden. Many may not have been tough enough to survive without special pampering, but some have been rediscovered growing in old gardens.

As the auricula primroses waned, new species were being introduced that captured the attention of gardeners. The Asiatic primroses were brighter and much easier to grow than the European Alpine kinds. The lavender Indian Drumstick, *Primula denticulata*, was introduced by the directors of the East India Company in 1842. The pale yellow *P. sikkimensis* came from the Himalayas in 1850. It was followed by the elegant candelabra species, *P. japonica, P. pulverulenta, P. helodoxa, P.*

bulleyana, and *P. beesiana.* Each has flowers arranged in whorls up the stems. Ever a nation of primrose-lovers, the English embraced the new immigrants, which still colonize watersides in many gardens.

BELOW, the tall spires of *Primula pulverulenta* 'Bartley Strain' are paired with *Astilbe × arendsii.* OVERLEAF, *Primula helodoxa,* LEFT, thrives at water's edge, while *P. bulleyana* and *P. beesiana,* RIGHT, bloom beneath shrubs.

CHAPTER TWO

A HISTORY
OF PERENNIAL
GARDENING
STYLES

"AMONG THE MANY FOLLIES which the gardening world commits, none is more striking to the looker-on, than the eagerness with which old favourites are deserted for new ones. Of all inconstant lovers, gardeners must surely be the most inconstant. In their eyes, old age is a crime, and aged flowers are mercilessly consigned to the poor house. If we look to an old garden catalogue, we can but wonder how the flower-garden was decorated by our fathers; for there we find little besides races now known only by name . . . or in remote country gardens, not yet reached by steam or electricity." From *The Gardener's Chronicle*, circa 1850.

Even in the seventeenth century, John Parkinson spoke of the vanished flowers of his youth, hoping they might still be found in isolated gardens. Since that time, there has been a steady, if unheeded, cry not to lose the flowers from the past. Even so, gardeners disposed of flowers that bored them. Some flowers survived despite sweeping changes in fashion, perhaps tended in secluded gardens. Others were swept in with a surge of enthusiasm, only to be abandoned in the next wave. An overview of English and American styles illustrates the dramatic evolution of ornamental gardening.

THE MIDDLE AGES

Late medieval gardens were simple affairs, based on those of the monasteries. Enclosed by rustic trellises and arbours, the garden was usually divided by paths into square sections. Wooden wattle fences often rimmed the edges. Meadows of flowers, called "flowery medes," like those depicted on old tapestries, were often incorporated. Grassy banks provided seating, the better to enjoy the predominantly aromatic plants of the day, including many herbs, roses, and fruiting bushes and trees. A quotation from Chaucer's translation of the *Roman de la rose* illuminates the garden of his day:

"Full gay was all the ground, and quaint,
And powdered, as men had it paint,
With many a fresh and sundry flower
That casten up full good savour."

Some may question whether "flower" and "savour" make a good rhyme (although it was a perfectly good rhyme in Middle English), but the importance of fragrant plants is evident. Remember, bathing was still not an everyday event.

Early gardeners favored roses and Feverfew, *Chrysanthemum parthenium*, FAR LEFT . Straight paths and wattle fences in an enclosed courtyard frame fruit trees surrounded by herbs and perennials, LEFT. Plants of the Mediterranean region, such as Lavender Cotton, *Santolina chamaecyparissus*, ABOVE, have played important roles in the garden for centuries.

THE SIXTEENTH CENTURY

By the sixteenth century gardening was a combination of practicality and decoration. Herbs were necessary, but beauty was considered too. The knot garden took England by storm. Low hedges were planted in interweaving patterns, and the strands within the knot were filled with bright blooms. New flowers were imported from the European mainland, including rarities discovered during the Spanish conquests in South America, as well as

often replaced by coloured stones, gravel, and coal dust.

This technique was frequently used when the knot represented a coat of arms, and the perennial edging plants, such as Lavender, Box, and Lavender Cotton, outlined patterns coloured with broken bricks, coloured chalk, or coal dust. The knots needed to be viewed from above to be fully appreciated, and were positioned to be seen from the upper floors of the

Perennials introduced to English gardens during the sixteenth century included Blue Alkanet, *Anchusa azurea*, ABOVE LEFT, and daylilies, *Hemerocallis*, ABOVE RIGHT, illustrated by 'Golden Chimes.' The knot garden, such as this one at the Barnsley House, RIGHT, gained favour during the same period.

from the Near East. New flowers introduced include daffodils, hyacinths, sunflowers, mallows, nasturtiums, and anchusas.

The knot garden patterns became more intricate over the next two hundred years. Of the elaborate garden of Thomas, Cardinal Wolsey, it was said it had "the knots so enknotted it cannot be expressed." The pattern became more important than the flowers within the design in many gardens. Indeed, the flowers were

house. Impressive as they must have been to most people, Francis Bacon jeered, "These be but toys: you may see as good sights many times in tarts."

During this period, North American colonial gardens were humble, reflecting only the need for "simples," the herbs for healing and cooking, and vegetables. It would be a hundred years until prosperity and stability allowed ornamental gardens to emerge in America.

AFTER THE RESTORATION

After the Restoration in 1660, English gardeners were influenced by the style set by Louis XIV's master gardener, André Le Nôtre. With Charles II on the throne, the gardens of Windsor Castle and Hampton Court were redesigned to resemble those of Versailles. (It has been said that never has so much money and manpower produced such a stingy effect as at Versailles.) The planting area within and around the old knot garden expanded and became the parterre, an ornamental garden with paths between the beds. The parterre could hold many more flowers, which were arriving quickly from foreign lands. The parterre was an Italian concept, copied first by the French—the word *parterre* was first used in France in 1549— and later by the English. Large gardens might feature a whole series of parterre gardens, divided by hedges or enclosed in elaborate mazes. The upkeep must have been staggering, what with all the trimming and weeding. Fortunately, the planting areas were filled with perennials— annual bedding plants, as we know them, did not exist. The display changed throughout the season as a succession of tulips, primroses, iris, and lilies came into bloom. Only the very rich could afford water works, clipped trees, and corridor hedges to accompany the new parterres.

The early Georgians seemed to have an aversion to having two of the same plants next to each other; and the formal beds were arranged "promiscuously," as the Victorians would later proclaim. They did, however, favour more than ample room between plants, so that plenty of earth showed. (Each of us probably has at least one neighbour who has inherited Georgian gardening sensibilities.) A new concept in gardening was developing on large properties where trees, shrubs, and grassy meadows were viewed from rough paths.

In North America, where they had plenty of wilderness, horticulture had begun to imitate the formal knots and parterres. The selection of available European plants was limited, and was supplemented by the rich native flora.

Many of these flowers from the New World were introduced to England by a father and son, both named John Tradescant. As a nurseryman and "Keeper of His Majesty's Gardens, Vines, and Silkworms" at Charles I's palace at Oatlands, John Senior had access to new plants arriving from abroad. He established a museum and garden of curiosities, which became known as Tradescant's Ark. (After the fall of the king, the family depended on the Ark for income.) He became a shareholder in the Virginia Company in 1617, having paid the passage for twenty-four settlers to the new colony. When new plants were shipped back to him, he shared them with his friend John Parkinson, who helped popularize them. The younger Tradescant visited Virginia first in 1637, bringing back many new plants. Between the two, such finds as Golden Rod, *Solidago canadensis*; Canadian Columbine, Cardinal Flower, *Lobelia cardinalis*; and Allegheny Foam Flower, *Tiarella cordifolia* were introduced. The Tradescants are commemorated by the purple Spiderwort, *Tradescantia virginiana*.

When the landscape movement began early in the eighteenth century, the new plants brought in for fashionable parterres disappeared from the gardens of the gentry as quickly as they had come. Fortunately many were kept and preserved in cottage gardens. Critics attacked the formal garden vigorously. Joseph Addison, writing in *The Spectator* in 1712, expressed the sentiment of the day, scolding British gardeners, who, ". . . instead of humouring Nature, love to deviate from it as much as possible. Our trees rise in cones, globes, pyramids. We see the marks of scissars [sic] on every plant and bush. I do not know whether I am singular in my opinion, but, for my own part, I would rather look upon a tree in all its Luxuriancy and Diffusion of boughs and branches than when it is thus cut and trimmed into a mathematical figure; and cannot but fancy an orchard in flower looks more delightful than all the labyrinths of the most finished parterre."

Addison was not "singular" in his opinion. Lancelot "Capability" Brown arrived on the scene, which he changed

The parterre was essentially an expansion of the knot garden as geometric beds were laid out with precision, inspired by the French example, after the Restoration in England. LEFT, beds of segregated roses echo the influence of the parterre.

considerably. The formal geometric plantings changed to "all natural" parks dotted with imitation temples and artificial lakes. Flowers were banished behind walls in kitchen gardens, or altogether, as the sophisticated gardener endeavoured to include the necessary clumps of shrubs and trees in parkland grazed by picturesque herds of deer or cattle, in an idyllic pastoral setting. The movement was disastrous for flowers, but it did teach designers to follow the natural features of the land, or as Alexander Pope stated, to "consult the genius of the place." The formal garden survived in remote areas, but the main business of growing flowers was left to the cottagers, whose gardens had become the last refuge of many plants discarded by the great houses.

The landscape garden never caught on in America as it had in England, although larger estates, such as those of George Washington and Thomas Jefferson, followed the dictates of the topography with informal plantings of trees and shrubs. There were few private estates that adopted the whole English landscape style, but the concepts were later embraced by the American parks movement, which built natural pleasure grounds for the public to enjoy. Formality still reigned in most private gardens, and despite the war of independence, horticultural ties between the two countries remained strong. American gardeners continued to order the latest plants from English nurseries.

The colonies of America, especially Virginia, provided a rich diversity of native plants that quickened the pulse of English gardeners. RIGHT, the Tradescants introduced many new plants like Goldenrod, *Solidago canadensis*.

It is ironic that towards the end of the century, Europeans developed a mad passion for American wildflowers, and fashion-conscious gardeners competed feverishly to collect new species. By the time of "Capability" Brown's death in 1783 there was a reaction against his landscapes, which were criticized for "the false and mistaken taste for placing a large house in a naked grass field without any apparent line of separation between the ground exposed to cattle and the ground annexed to the house." The words belong to Humphrey Repton, the most exclusive garden designer in England after Brown,

who restored the flower garden to prominence. It had never really vanished, of course, and flowers had remained in the smaller manor houses and vicarages, where good sense or lack of money had kept the owners from ploughing under their gardens. Bernard McMahon, perhaps inspired by Repton, initiated the "gardenesque" style in America. McMahon's *The American Gardener's Calender*, from 1806, was the country's first important book on horticulture and landscape design. The gardenesque style featured "rural open spaces" planted with thickets of trees and bushes, and separate formal areas for growing flowers.

ABOVE, the stalks of cream-coloured flowers rise above the jagged lobes of the leaves of *Rodgersia podophylla*, which take on a bronze tone as they mature; burgundy foliage and roses form a handsome backdrop.

EARLY PLANT HUNTING

English plant-hunting expeditions, which date back at least to the Crusades, intensified during the eighteenth century. Sir Joseph Banks, who had sailed with Captain James Cook on his first voyage, inspired George III to turn the gardens at Kew House, originally a private estate, into an exchange centre for important commercial plants. (Instigated by Banks, the original voyage to transfer the Breadfruit Tree to the West Indies from islands in the South Seas was aboard the *H.M.S. Bounty*, Captain William Bligh commanding. The famed mutiny delayed the completion of the project until 1793, by which time the French had already established the trees in Martinique. Breadfruit never became the important crop the English had hoped.) Banks was determined that Kew should become the world centre of botanical research. Collectors were sent out to supply His Majesty's Botanic Garden with plants heretofore unseen in the west. Official collectors were dispatched to southern Africa, Brazil, and Australia. The East India Company also sent specimens.

Plant hunting was a dangerous business. Japan and China were reluctant to open their doors to foreigners, and those that were admitted lived in peril of bandits, floods, and sickness. The job was often a thankless one—the discoverer of the noble *Rodgersia podophylla* from Japan went unrecorded. French missionaries, many of whom were also botanists, were persecuted in China; some escaped by disguising themselves as beggars.

Pierre-Nicholas d'Incarville was dispatched in 1739 by the Jesuits with the mission of converting the emperor of China to Christianity. In this he failed, but he shipped many new species home, despite the shipwreck of one shipment and the theft of another by the British. Many of d'Incarville's packets were set aside in Paris and rediscovered many years later, unopened. The same fate later befell many of the 200,000 specimens, including 1,500 new species, sent to the French Natural History Museum by Jean-Marie Delavay. This missionary explored Yunnan, the southwestern province of China near Burma, in the late nineteenth century. About the same time, Abbé Armand David, the French priest who was the first Westerner to see a panda, collected plants in Inner Mongolia. (The beautiful little native deer of the region, which are extinct in the wild, are called Père David's deer. They survived at Woburn and are being reintroduced to their native land.)

Losses were heavy when plants were shipped home. Dutch, English, and French ships regularly hijacked each other's plant cargoes. Many were eaten by rats, were killed by salt spray, or simply rotted before reaching their final destination. Upon arrival, conventional wisdom often decreed that plants from exotic lands would survive in stove houses. Plants from temperate climates promptly died from this kindness. The Wardian case, a portable glass terrarium, was invented in 1829. It greatly improved the odds of plants' survival on long ocean voyages. The technological advances in affordable glass and iron of the Industrial Revolution made greenhouses as we know them possible.

VICTORIAN GARDENING STYLES

By the time Victoria ascended the British throne in 1837, garden fashion had swung full circle, and geometric beds were back. The grandest homes echoed the Italianate parterres of the Continent, and except for the cottage gardens, every garden was filled to the brim with statues, urns, fountains, and hedges. Bedding schemes ruled the day. In times past, older plants had gradually fallen from favour. The Victorians, who had the luxury of greenhouses and legions of plant hunters combing the globe, shed their castoffs with a vengeance. Ribbon bedding often utilized hothouse-grown annuals in bands of bright colours, frequently in scrolls or the Greek key patterns. Parterres were often filled with similarly coloured plantings, commonly accented with a dot plant in the centre of each bed. The true carpet bedding was exactly that, an intricate imitation of the Oriental and Caucasian rugs that were all the rage. Carpet beds were almost always made from foliage plants pinched and carefully trimmed, and some were subtle and sophisticated, despite the general reputation to the contrary of many from the period. Annuals ruled the day. The perennials that could be adapted to the bedding schemes were favoured and the rest were largely ignored.

For the first time, nursery catalogues were printed with prices listed. Formerly, estate owners would negotiate privately for plants and bulbs. The new priced lists indicated an increasing gardening public of the middle class.

Women became more and more involved in horticultural activity, as it was considered a proper pastime for the well-bred lady. Joseph Breck reflected the American attitude in 1851, when he wrote, "The cultivation and study of flowers appears more suited to females than to man. They resemble them in their fragility, beauty, and perishable nature. The Mimosa may be likened to a pure-minded and delicate woman, who shrinks even from the breath of contamination; and who, if assailed too rudely by the finger of scorn and reproach, will wither and die from the shock." (Little is known about Mrs. Breck; the Mimosa is seldom grown today.)

Change was in the wind, however, and blew in like a gale in the form of William Robinson. He railed incessantly against the bedding schemes. His book, *The English Flower Garden*, first published in 1883, inspired a revolution in style and is a classic today. He considered geometric beds filled with a single greenhouse-grown species not only "pastry-cooks' work," but degrading to the individual plants. He proposed that the lines between cultivated and wild plants be less marked, and first suggested how bulbs and wildflowers might be naturalized where they might take care of themselves best in orchards and woods, and on hillsides. Where Brown's "natural" style had driven the flower garden out, Robinson's flower garden of hardy perennials tumbled off the terrace and into the countryside. As his arguments were slowly heeded, bedding schemes disappeared or new herbaceous perennial borders were incorporated to coexist with them. Sometimes these became gaudy and ostentatious too.

THE QUEST FOR EXOTICS

Exploration continued for plants around the world. The Horticultural Society of London sent David Douglas to gather seeds and plants in the American West. He introduced over two hundred species, many of which had originally been discovered during the expedition of Meriwether Lewis and William Clark in 1803. Their attempt to find a waterway passage between the Atlantic and Pacific coasts was foiled by the Rocky Mountains, but they discovered many new flowers, among them *Gaillardia aristata*, known for its bright hues as Indian Blanket.

The Victorians, for all their skill in the greenhouse, were astonishingly unsophisticated in their knowledge of soils and drainage; many a western flower perished in a boggy bed.

The Horticultural Society of London sent Robert Fortune to China in 1842. He was instructed not to bring home anything that needed coddling in the greenhouse, unless it was really special. China had been forced to reopen its doors following the Opium War of 1839–1842 (Britain took the Chinese ban on the importation of the drug as a pretext to force an end to restrictions on foreign trade in general), but travel was still restricted and perilous. Fortune lived up to his name, and returned with hundreds of new plants. Two of the most important, however, had already been introduced but lost. Upon their reintroduction, Balloon Flower, *Platycodon grandiflorus*, and Bleeding Heart, *Dicentra spectabilis*, became overnight sensations. In another expedition, the famous nursery firm Veitch sent collector William Lobb to South America in 1840. He secured abundant supplies of seed of the Monkey Puzzle Tree in Argentina, and seeds of *Abutilon vitifolium*, the so-called Flowering Maple from Chile.

A Monkey Puzzle Tree, *Araucaria imbricata*, hangs over a bed, ABOVE. BELOW, *Gaillardia aristata* was discovered by Lewis and Clark. *Abutilon vitifolium* thrives against a wall, OPPOSITE.

TWENTIETH-CENTURY STYLE AND BEYOND

The gardens of the twentieth century have been heavily influenced by Gertrude Jekyll, who in collaboration with the architect Sir Edwin Lutyens designed gardens of beauty unequalled before or since. The perennial border was essentially redrawn, and certainly recoloured by the pair, who met in 1889. Miss Jekyll was influenced not only by William Robinson, but by the paintings of the Impressionists, and her friend Maria Theresa Earle, who under the name of Mrs. C. W. Earle wrote of her admiration of the simplicity of cottage gardens. In the United States, Beatrix Ferrand, who designed Dumbarton Oaks, helped to reshape gardens as did Frederick Law Olmsted, who left a legacy of magnificent public parks. Their works, which combined formal and informal elements, affected public perceptions about gardening styles, and inspired the transition from the Victorian gaudiness to a subtler palette.

Gardens of today are varied, as they reflect their local climate, architectural styles, and ethnic influences. Native plants are often incorporated with traditional ones, or planted exclusively. The latter approach is a narrow one, ignoring the adaptable perennials gathered from far lands of like climates. Gardens evolve, and each gardener must seek the style that suits his or her site and temperament. Thalassa Cruso is an Englishwoman transplanted to Massachusetts soil whose *Making Things Grow Outdoors* taught a generation. She urges people to know themselves before they plan a garden, saying, "Obses-

The formal design of a herb garden, ABOVE, echoes the past. Terraces of stone, OPPOSITE ABOVE, are softened by Siberian iris, pinks, Snow-in-summer, and Catnip. *Cimicifuga racemosa* towers above yarrow, *Platycodon*, and Lamb's-ears, OPPOSITE BELOW.

sively tidy gardeners are better off with something informal; otherwise every weed or unswept leaf will seem like a personal affront needing immediate action." She continues, "But in case your temperament outdoors is a mystery to you, think in terms of your reaction as a housekeeper. If you empty the ashtrays while your friends are still smoking, you will be equally bothered by weeds in the yard, and you will be better off with a style of garden that doesn't show them up." She further advises, "If you are a casual housekeeper, go right ahead and lay out brick terraces and clipped walks, for you will enjoy them even when you know that you ought to do something about their appearance."

The reconstruction and renovation of period gardens is a new gardening phenomenon, and only recently has there been an attempt to plant authentic plants in period gardens. Those wishing to recreate or interpret a garden appropriate to the age of their house may wish to check the date of introduction of any given variety they choose to plant. Many who take great pains to furnish their homes with fine antiques, and would never even consider putting a Danish modern table beside a Queen Anne chair, plant frilly petunias and hybrid tea roses in their gardens without a thought. There is nothing wrong with this, of course, although to exclude the antique flowers is to deprive oneself of the very pleasures that come from living with the styles of the past. Even without a two-hundred-year-old farmhouse, or rooms full of Sheridan furniture, any gardener may delight in growing the plants from the past and learning their histories.

CHAPTER THREE

A PORTFOLIO OF
ANTIQUE
PERENNIALS

Acanthus Acanthaceae

Acanthus, native to Asia minor, is a stately and architecturally structured plant of great antiquity. According to legend, the Greek sculptor Callimachus was so moved by the sight of the leaf of acanthus on a child's grave, he was inspired to use its pattern on the capital of a new column—the Corinthian—he had in mind. This happened in the fifth century B.C., and I find the account a bit suspect. Quite frankly, it takes a stretch of the imagination to see an acanthus leaf in a Corinthian capital. I hasten to point out that I am not a scholar of Greek art, but as a student I was required to memorize the Ionic, Doric, and Corinthian columns, and as a gardener I am confused. The acanthus in my garden and the leaves depicted on the capital do not match. Those designs look like leaves of some sort, but it's difficult to say that they are not just any old thistle.

The Greeks would have been aware of the prickly spines of the leaves. The name is derived from *akantha*, which is Greek for thorn. There are two prominent members of the genus found in Asia Minor, but the plant with leaves most resembling Callimachus' version is *A. mollis*, Smooth Acanthus. This species grows only in damp places in northern Greece, and it is unlikely he would have seen it first-hand so far south as Corinth. It is likely he modified a design already in use, perhaps originating in Macedonia.

The common name for *Acanthus* is Bear's Breeches, which has also inspired some improbable theories about its origin.

Acanthus mollis
SMOOTH ACANTHUS
Acanthus spinosus
BEAR'S BREECHES

The flowers of *Acanthus spinosus* are of architectural interest in a planting, OPPOSITE. ABOVE, spikes of acanthus are combined with *Origananum libanoticum*, *Rubus odoratus*, and *Astrantia major* in a subdued arrangement.

The leaves have alternatively been described as resembling the matted hair on a bear or appropriate apparel for this ferocious animal. *A. mollis* was cultivated in England as early as the thirteenth century. Early gardening literature, including John Parkinson's *Paradisus* (1629) and Gerard's *Herball* (1597), accepted the name "Bear's Breech" and made no attempt to explain.

A. spinosus, Spiny Acanthus, was introduced into England in 1629. It is an imposing plant, not only for the handsome, dark green leaves, but for the stiff spike flowers that reach four to five feet (1.2–1.5m) in height. The pale mauve flowers are clustered in bracts along the stem. Once the flowers have faded, they are replaced by seed pods nestled in the purple calyxes. The seeds turn dark brown, and the entire stem can be dried for arrangements but one must take pains, so to speak, to avoid the sharp points of the calyx. *A. mollis* is similar in stature and flower, although the leaves have a dull finish, rather than the polished sheen of Spiny Acanthus, and feature deeply cut lobes. There are subspecies and apparently very old hybrids between the two, which explains the variation in the degrees of lobing and spininess of the foliage encountered in some plants.

Since it flowers less freely, and is less hardy, Smooth Acanthus is less frequently grown. Both prosper in fertile, well-drained soil and flower best in sun, although they can be grown in partial shade. Spiny Acanthus may succeed in cold climates, given some initial coddling, especially in regard to drainage and proper protection. Under these conditions, it may make large clumps, and become aggressive with its invasive roots.

Where to place *Acanthus* in the garden depends on aesthetics. Despite its height, Bear's Breeches can be shown to advantage near, or at the front of, a border. Its dark and sombre nature can be underscored by companion plants with less bold foliage, and flowers of similar mauve hues. Veronicas and the shrubby veronicas (which are now classified as *Hebe*), hardy geraniums, and *Dictamnus* associate well. Such burgundy-leaved shrubs as *Rosa rubrifolia* and *Cotinus coggygria*, or Smoke Tree, top the list of well-chosen backdrops.

According to legend, the wise centaur Chiron first told Achilles how to use the leaves of this herb to treat his injured soldiers during the siege of Troy. Strangely, and perhaps unfairly, it was named *Achillea*, not *Chironia*. Its use as a wound-herb continued for many centuries, and is reflected by folk names like Staunchgrass, Woundwort, and Bloodwort. "Yarrow" is commonly accepted now, derived from an old Anglo-Saxon word *gearwe*, which meant "ready to heal."

Two species of *Achillea* are native to northern Europe, and have been naturalized in parts of America. *A. millefolium*, the Common Yarrow, is cursed as a lawn weed, but the red deviations from the standard white form have long been found in gardens. Gerard mentions discovering a crimson form growing wild. It is these naturally occurring sports that were adopted by cottage gardeners. The feathery green leaves, which give it the country name of Milfoil (thousand-leafed), support milky-pink heads in great profusion. In folklore, it was considered one of the

witches' herbs. Well-wishers brought bunches of Venus's-tree, as it was also called, to weddings to ensure seven years of true love. (Presumably, the couple were on their own after that, which suggests a medieval seven-year itch.) Milfoil had medicinal applications as well, and was used to treat boils, bronchitis, toothaches,

and flatulence. It was also called Nosebleed, but whether it cured them or caused them is not always clear. Gerard wrote, "The leaves being put into the nose, do cause it to bleed and easeth the pain of the megrim." Perhaps this procedure was used when leeches were not to be had.

The other wild sort of yarrow, *A.*

A. filipendulina floats in front of clumps of *Lychnis chalcedonica* and *Thalictrum speciosissimum*,
LEFT. ILLUSTRATION, TOP, and ABOVE, pink forms of *A. millefolium* occur naturally.

Achillea Compositae

Achillea filipendulina GOLDEN YARROW

Achillea millefolium NOSEBLEED

Achillea ptarmica SNEEZEWORT

The lofty golden plates of *A. filipendulina* bloom, ABOVE. A tureen holds *A. filipendulina*, dill, *Epilobium angustifolium*, and the white *Physostegia virginiana*, BELOW RIGHT.

intense colours. My choice would be to group it with masses of other yellows, from canary marguerites to creamy meadowsweets. The flowers hold their colour well when dried, and have been used for so long this way that they are almost a cliché. My advice here is to throw them out before they disappear behind cobwebs.

It may be a surprise to learn that yarrows are classified as part of Compositae, the daisy family. Close inspection will reveal clusters of small daisylike flowers without the petals. The flower heads are borne on strong stems that branch at the top. The twiggy branches culminate in a full, flat head.

The achilleas are among the most accommodating of garden flowers. They are not fussy about soil or water. Full sun is preferred; otherwise the golden heads of

The pure white form of *A. ptarmica*, ABOVE, was first raised in 1850 and is now known as 'The Pearl'. A sea of yellow, RIGHT, is created by *A. filipendulina* and annual sunflowers.

ptarmica, is also a native of Europe. It was known as White Pellitory or Sneezewort, since the leaves were powdered and used for snuff, especially to relieve headaches. Double-flowered forms, cultivated by the sixteenth century, were called Shirtbuttons. The famous French nurseryman Victor Lemoine raised a clean white double around 1850, originally called 'Boule de Neige'; we know it as 'The Pearl.' In the spectrum of white flowers, most have a hint of blue, green, pink, or cream, but 'The Pearl' is pure white.

The best-known of the yarrows is *A. filipendulina*, introduced to England from Central Europe in 1803. The golden heads are about five inches (13cm) across, and float like saucers over clumps of fine aromatic foliage. A huge clump is a fine sight, especially grouped with flowers of equally

A. filipendulina will flop. Yarrows are remarkably free of pests and plagues, and with this iron-clad constitution they can be aggressive to a fault. Milfoil is especially vigorous, and I have to get in and hack at it every so often. The divisions are easily transplanted. A radical haircut in midsummer will rejuvenate it, stimulating fresh blooms for the autumn.

As gardeners, we sometimes turn up our noses at these common plants, choosing instead to throw money and effort into novelties that have no intentions of persisting in our gardens. I am certainly not advocating that we stop experimenting, only that we don't dismiss a good plant just because it grows well. Familiarity need not breed contempt. The achilleas, after decades of contempt, are finally becoming respectable again.

Aconitum
Ranunculaceae

Aconitum anthora YELLOW WOLF'S BANE

Aconitum napellus MONKSHOOD

Cultivated since the sixteenth century, *Aconitum napellus* is native to parts of Europe, including Britain, and Asia. In past ages, a future as a garden flower seemed unlikely for this plant; the pollen was used on the tips of poison arrows, and the Greeks and Romans laced bait with the roots to kill wolves. Country people called it Wolf's Bane. The Latin name has been linked to the hill Aconitus, where, in one version of the story, Hercules battled Cerberus, the three-headed dog guarding the gate of Hades. Its rabid foam fell to the ground, and the poisonous flowers sprang up. Shakespeare spoke of "aconitum" in *King Henry IV (Part II)*, comparing the strength of its poison to gunpowder. Even so, the plant became a popular one, though Turner, a contemporary of Shakespeare's, wrote, "Let our Londoners which of late have received this blew wolfs' bayne, otherwyse called Monkes-coule, take hede. . . ."

The hooded flowers have captured the imagination for a very long time. "Granny's-nightcap," "Captain-over-the-Garden," "Chariot-and-horses," and "Helmet Flower" are among the folk names it has been given. Writers of every period continually warned of its dangers. Gerard relates "a lamentable example at Antwerp," where the tender young leaves were "by certaine ignorant persons served up in sallads, all that did eat thereof were presently taken with most cruell symptomes, and so died." Linnaeus told of an incompetent doctor who prescribed the leaves for a patient who refused to take them (perhaps he had perused Gerard's *Herball* in the waiting room). To reassure the man, the doctor ingested them himself,

ABOVE and RIGHT, sombre spires of Monkshood, *Aconitum napellus*, have been grown in English gardens since the sixteenth century, despite the plants' poisonous nature.

with fatal results. Both of these gruesome tales came from the Continent, however, and English gardeners could not fathom such stupidity. To cast Monkshood out of the garden would be, as Victorian writer Benjamin Maund put it, "rather fastidious, inasmuch as the English are not so

Despite its pretty pale flowers and its repute as an antidote for the poison of the other species, *Aconitum anthora*, ABOVE, is rarely grown. OPPOSITE, an old china pitcher holds stems of *Aconitum napellus* 'Spark's Variety', Larkspur, *Consolida ambigua*, Plumed thistle, *Cirsium japonicum*, and oak leaves.

passionately attached to a vegetable diet as to eat garden herbage indiscriminately." Besides, the plant was a useful one. It enjoyed a reputation for solving unhappy marriages, although it was considered rather a vulgar remedy—not at all the sort of poison for a person of good

breeding. It was also said to be a cure for lycanthropy, but I cannot attest to the fact.

Disrepute aside, gardeners valued Monkshood for its beauty. The denim-blue flowers are enhanced by darker veins, almost brown, which create a subtle overall impression of purple. The key word is subtle, since the hue is a dark, not a vivid, one. The floral spires of *A. napellus* reach four or five feet (1.2 or 1.5m) and stay in bloom for three weeks or more. They rarely need staking, even when grown in shade. Graham Stuart Thomas, the eminent British plantsman, notes, ". . . full sun suits them though they will also grow well in part or full shade—when the darkened colours of some kinds appear to increase in their evil beauty." Since the monkshoods are members of Ranunculaceae, the buttercup tribe, it is not surprising this plant thrives in a moisture-retentive soil. The leaves are dark and deeply cut, and emerge early in the spring.

Late in the last century, 'Spark's Variety' was introduced, with its intense violet-blue flowers, and 'Bicolor' is an old garden hybrid with white and blue coloration. The native English species, *A. anglicum*, has been grown for many centuries, and differs primarily from *A. napellus* by blooming earlier in the summer. The wild American species, found throughout the Rocky Mountains, is *A. columbianum*, which is shorter and has flowers with a vivid violet cast. An unusual species, *A. vulparia*, is noted for pale yellow flowers of which the Victorians were fond. One other yellow member of the genus, *A. anthora*, is reputed to be an antidote to all the others, but inexplicably has never been grown widely in gardens, and is very rare. I grow

it not as a remedy, but for its two-foot (60cm) spikes of pale flowers that associate so well with lavender-pink astilbes.

Monkshood is an excellent, though often overlooked, garden subject. We live in a gardening culture that values delphiniums more highly. I contend that any plant that has been bred to fall over, such as the modern delphinium, cannot impart any real grace to the garden (despite all attempts at inconspicuous staking, which is a contradiction in terms). This is not to imply that this plant may not be worth the trouble, except that this Johnny-come-lately to the garden has overshadowed the ancient and venerable *Aconitum*. To the breeders of the twentieth century, a plant called Monkshood, or worse, Wolf's Bane, must have seemed decidedly outmoded. That is a shame, since in the garden, *Aconitum* is irreplaceable. Their sombre tone is just the thing to pair with crimson roses that often are shadowed with a bluish cast as they mature. Fine, too, are combinations with the golden yellows of *Anthemis, Heliopsis*, or *Rudbeckia*. To my mind, the pale indigo blooms look their best borne against Dusty Meadow Rue, *Thalictrum speciosissimum*.

Of late, Monkshood has begun to appear at florist's shops. It has a long vase life, but cannot be recommended for the dining table. Recently I ate in a London restaurant where huge bunches of Monkshood decorated each table. Encouraged as I was to see one of my favourite flowers displayed so lavishly, I worried through my entire meal that a blossom might fall in an unsuspecting patron's salad. I checked mine over thoroughly. Londoners, take hede. . . .

Edward A. Bowles, a turn-of-the-century gardener, with a keen sense of observation, noted that the leaves of *Alchemilla mollis* are ". . . of a very tender shade of greyish-green and covered with fine, silky hairs which help their cup-like shape to hold raindrops glittering like drops of quick-silver." If anyone thinks that this is strictly an English phenomenon, I can assure them that the same occurs in my Denver garden. Few sights are as lovely as the dew trapped on the leaves of Lady's Mantle in the morning. Many a garden writer has praised this plant since its introduction from Turkey in 1874; yet it is still too seldom seen. Perhaps it is because the flowers are so small—tiny chartreuse sprays—that it has been overlooked by gardeners. Once I was particularly im-pressed by a rose bed. Walking down the grass path, I thought I had never seen such vivid and luscious blooms—seashell pinks, delicate corals, and frosted raspberries. I realized the colours appeared so rich because they floated on a sea of chartreuse. Lady's Mantle lined the edge of each bed, and had seeded among the rose bushes. Whether by plan or by chance, the owner was wise to accept the volunteers. Visitors might notice only the roses (though they'd have to be quite insensitive to have missed this splendid pairing) and decide simply to plant more roses. That, of course, they could do. What they would have is a lot more roses, but without the effect.

A friend of mine, who is a very talented flower arranger, swears by it for enlivening a bouquet. The peculiar colour of the

Alchemilla mollis
Rosaceae

LADY'S MANTLE

flowers is a remarkable foil for blossoms of lavender, pink, white, and blue, without drawing too much attention to itself. The downy, rounded leaves are equally valuable in arrangements, especially with pale peach and cream.

The pleated leaves were thought to resemble an old-fashioned cloak, which may explain the common name. A more plausible theory suggests the wild species, *A. vulgaris*, was consecrated by monks to Mary, and was originally "Our Lady's Mantle." Old herbals confirm the name was in use by 1548. It should be noted that the two species are very similar, and *A. vulgaris* is broken down into more than twenty subspecies found growing in Europe. Gardeners need not worry about the differences, though, as most plants sold under the name *A. vulgaris* are most likely *A. mollis*. At the other extreme, some imagined enough of a resemblance to call it Lion's Foot. The drops of water trapped on the leaves were collected (fruitlessly, I suppose) by generations of frustrated alchemists; the Latin name alludes to this pursuit of easy money.

Alchemilla was also respected for its medicinal values. Nicholas Culpeper published his *Complete Herbal* in 1652; he recommends internal and external use of Lady's Mantle for a variety of female troubles. Two daily cups of Lady's Mantle tea were thought advisable during pregnancy. He also commended its use for treating wounds, "for it dries up the humidity of sores, and heals inflammation."

A. mollis may grow to a height of eighteen inches (45cm) while in flower, although the foliage hugs the ground. It is the largest species of a genus that occurs throughout parts of Europe and western Asia. Most are diminutive plants but some, like *A. alpina*, are substantial enough for the perennial garden. All, happily, offer decorative foliage and feathery sprays of flowers. The gardens at Cambridge University have an entire bed devoted to the many species of *Alchemilla*.

Lady's Mantle is not difficult to grow. It prefers moist soil with a bit of sun, but will perform adequately in a wide variety of conditions and soils. It takes unkindly to draught, and under such stress will inevitably develop a severe case of spider mites.

Some books claim that Lady's Mantle is a nuisance, seeding itself with great abandon. Others have a more tolerant approach, implying a garden can almost never have too much *Alchemilla* until you find you have nothing else. Margery Fish, a twentieth-century gardener with eighteenth-century sensibilities, thought too much of a good thing was wonderful. She wrote, "It is a persistent seeder but it always seems to find places where it looks best—at the bottom of a wall or in a bare corner where there is hardly room for its roots. I never mind how many seedlings I find in the garden, for they are all welcome." I'm not lucky enough to have all these wonderful weeds in my garden, having to rely on division to increase my stock. In a more favourable climate, remove the spent flower heads before the seed ripens, or plant the volunteers beneath your roses.

Sprays of chartreuse blossoms are held above a clump of *Alchemilla mollis*, OPPOSITE ABOVE. Downy leaves of Lady's Mantle accent Montbretia, *Crocosmia × crocosmiiflora*, and roses, OPPOSITE BELOW. BELOW, Lady's Mantle edges Lupin and Fennel.

Allium Amaryllidaceae

Allium cernuum NODDING ONION

Allium christophii STARS-OF-PERSIA

Allium senescens TUFTED CHIVES

Allium tuberosum CHINESE CHIVES

The onion has found a place in gardens since the earliest civilizations. The genus name may be derived from the Celtic *all*, meaning "hot" or "burning," alluding to the well-known gastronomic qualities of these plants. During the Middle Ages, onions were used variously to improve vision, treat dog bites, counteract baldness, and remove blemishes. Not only that, they were said to improve sexual prowess, any unpleasant breath not withstanding. The ornamental value of some alliums has been less appreciated, although with such virtues this may hardly seem important. Peter Henderson, one of America's leading plantsmen a hundred years ago, lamented, "Of the one hundred and fifty species of the tribe, but few are considered ornamental; indeed, the family, probably from prejudice, has been much neglected, where far less showy plants have found favor."

Common chives, garlic, leeks, and onions have always been included in the kitchen garden, but the prettier sorts have never found such continuous favour, with the possible exception of the freakish *A. giganteum*, which impressed the later Victorians and continues to be a staple of autumn bulb catalogues. Even so, some alliums were featured in Elizabethan gardens, especially the Golden Garlic, *A. moly*, and all the ornamental types became known as mollies. The dainty lavender flower heads of *A. senescens*, Tufted Chives, are accented by bluish clumps of curled narrow leaves. *A. tuberosum*, Chinese Chives, was imported from the Far East during the frenzy of plant explorations

following the end of the Opium Wars. It is edible and pretty. Each chalk-white blossom has a dark eye. The flower heads grow on stems up to eighteen inches (45cm) high, and are at their best in late summer. The scent and taste of chives are due to their sulphur-rich oils.

Discriminating English gardeners embraced the Nodding Onion, *A. cernuum*, when it was introduced about 1800 from America. There is no question that these flowers with their drooping heads on six-inch (15cm) stems are the most charming of the lot. The sprays of flowers give the effect of exploding firecrackers. The colour

A drift of the amethyst-pink flower heads of the North American native Nodding Onion, *Allium cernuum*, tumbles down a rocky bank, OPPOSITE. BELOW, the spherical lavender heads of Stars-of-Persia, *Allium christophii*, are a pleasing counterpart to the slender spikes of Purple Toadflax, *Linaria purpurea*.

is a choice one; it might be described as soft amethyst pink. Drifts of the nodding heads are lovely all by themselves on a bank or slope. They are useful for edging, and the subtle colour shows to advantage against the lacy grey foliage of Partridge Feather, *Tanacetum densum*, or the pale green spikes of *Ballota pseudodictamnus*. After its early summer display, the seed heads are also attractive.

The Turkish *A. christophii* (syn. *A. albopilosum*) has the largest head, about ten inches (25cm) across. Despite its colossal size, it is far from vulgar. The leaves have already died down in June when the spheres of pale violet stars—they are sometimes called Stars-of-Persia—open on their short stalks. The centre of each starry flower is later studded with a green seed capsule. The round heads last well, and as might be imagined, are marvellous for arranging when dry. To avoid patches of bare earth when the leaves die, clumps of *A. christophii* may be overplanted with pansies in the autumn, or grown through a shallow-rooted groundcover like *Veronica filiformis*, Bird's-eye Veronica. The mat of tiny leaves will not prevent the stout stems from emerging, and will carpet the soil with delicate pale blue flowers in spring.

None of these ornamental onions are difficult; all require only average soil and sunny conditions and are quite hardy. One related plant that is more suited for warmer gardens is *Tulbaghia violacea*, otherwise known as Society Garlic. This South African native was first grown in England in 1838, and became a feature of Victorian gardens. The pink bells hang from a tight umbel, and have no telltale onion scent.

Alstroemeria
Alstroemeriaceae

Alstromeria aurantiaca PERUVIAN LILY

Alstromeria ligtu

Spanish conquistadors were the first Europeans to see the *Alstroemeria*, christening it the Lily of the Incas. Also called lily of Peru, and laughingly "Chile lily," the *Alstroemeria* is not a true lily, being more closely related to the amaryllis. Spanish missionaries sent seeds from South America to their homelands. The first species in Europe was *A. pelegrina*. The botanical name honours Baron Claes Alströmer, who spotted the lavender flowers in 1753 in a garden in Cadiz, and sent seed to his friend Carolus Linnaeus. The Father of Botany repaid the debt by immortalizing his friend's name, if misspelling it. Linnaeus was so taken with the description of the flowers, that he nursed his young seedlings through the winter in his bedroom to ensure their survival.

Linnaeus' species was grown the next year in England, and was followed in 1776 by *A. caryophyllaea*, from Brazil, which at that time was called *A. ligtu*. *Ligtu* is the Indian name for the *Alstroemeria*. (To confuse matters, there is a true *A. ligtu*, which came into cultivation some forty years later.) *A. caryophyllaea* is scented, a fact denoted by the species name, which alludes to the Carnation, *Dianthus caryophyllus*.

A few more species trickled into England at the beginning of the nineteenth century. *A. aurantiaca*, with golden orange flowers, the real *A. ligtu*, in shades of red, and *A. haemantha*, orange and yellow with maroon markings, were soon popular greenhouse subjects. It was found that seeds were apt to produce a variety of colours, and hybridization was easy. *A. ligtu* was the most difficult to grow, but its genes imparted delicate peach and pink tints to the hybrids. The dark markings, borrowed largely from *A. haemantha*, are wonderfully evolved to attract insects. As if painted with a fine brush and steady hand, they provide a perfect landing blueprint for the moths that pollinate the species in its native habitat.

Flower clusters of the Peruvian Lilies, often a half dozen or more depending on the species, are held above whorls of thick grassy leaves. These leaves are unique among garden flowers, to my knowledge, in that they are held upside down. Each leaf twists at the point where it projects from the stem, bringing what should have been the bottom to the top. Curious gardeners, by bending over young stalks, have persuaded the leaves to make a second twist to keep the underside towards the light. It is small wonder that alstroemerias have long fascinated artistic gardeners and arrangers.

It is thanks to the florist trade that this native of the Andes has enjoyed a resurgence of interest. I was invited recently to enter a flower arrangement at a big show, where classes have "themes." My theme had to do with the golden age of colonial Cuzco. Rising to the challenge, I filled a brass urn with all sorts of gold and crimson flowers, dominated by a mass of alstroemerias. This ancient flower, one of the few I could think of that originated from Peru, has recently become a trendy cut flower. In the absence of true inspiration, I hoped the judges would be swayed by the authenticity of my floral choices. I'm positive they were impressed, and

The Peruvian Lily, **A.** *aurantiaca*, ILLUSTRATION, OPPOSITE, is easily hybridized with other species. OPPOSITE ABOVE, **A.** *ligtu* hybrids grow near a doorway. OPPOSITE BELOW, maroon markings attract insects. A boiler of Peruvian Lilies, ABOVE, makes a focal point.

insisted on rewarding the most beautiful bouquet—it was not mine.

The golden orange Peruvian Lily, *A. aurantiaca*, has proved to be a good garden subject once the finer points of its culture were worked out. Mrs. C. W. Earle, in her 1897 *Pot-pourri from a Surrey Garden*, advised that, "They do not mind moving in August after flowering, and they are best increased as Lilies of the Valley are—by digging out square pieces, filling in with good soil and dropping in the pieces cut out where they are wanted . . . without disturbing the earth that clings to them." Her suggestions are still valid. Sandy loam and moderate moisture serve them best, and young

plants need winter protection. Hardiness is variable, and in America successes have been reported as far north as Philadelphia. Once established, the plants are self-sufficient, and in mild areas the roots may run very deep and cannot be eradicated without great effort and a backhoe. In areas of cold winters, these can be stored in frost-free places while the plants are dormant. Young foliage is a bright green, and the floral fireworks begin in June, lasting well into July. Alstroemerias last for up to two weeks in water, with the buds continuing to open. They do not, however, guarantee a blue ribbon.

It is not flashy; it is not showy. Yet it is a particular favourite of a handful of gardeners, though a subject of great indifference to others. Margery Fish was among the former. Singing the praises of *Astrantia*, she said, "The present interest in astrantias is just another example of the uncanny way the cottagers had of finding and keeping a good plant. These flowers have been grown for many years in cottage gardens, and they looked perfectly at home there. Now other people are discovering how beautiful they are. . . . They fit in so well with our informal mixed borders and are the perfect plants to grow with shrubs; they are, in fact, the best of good mixers." The astrantias have been mixing it up in English gardens since 1597, when they were imported from their native Austria and Switzerland, where they are found growing wild at the edge of woodlands and in alpine meadows.

The best-known species is *Astrantia major*, which has distinct and beautiful flowers. Each flower head has a tiny cluster of florets, arranged in a dome, surrounded by a collar of petal-like bracts. One of the old names was Hattie's Pincushion, and the image has merit. The collars are pale green and a white flushed with varying degrees of pink. The species is variable, and some selected varieties have longer collars, and others have a dusky plum colouring. The colouring of all the astrantias is subtle; perhaps this led to the old country name of Melancholy Gentleman. There is nothing melancholy about them, as far as I'm concerned.

Astrantia major
Umbelliferae

HATTIE'S PINCUSHION

The delicately coloured flowers of Hattie's Pincushion, *Astrantia major*, are refined companions for many plants, as shown, LEFT, with the buds of the Turk's-cap Lily, *Lilium martagon*. ABOVE, the blossoms of *Astrantia major* owe their distinct look to the collar of bracts known as the involucre, and a dome of ray florets that resemble pins.

A selection that Mrs. Fish, who almost single-handedly inspired the antique plant movement, rescued from an old garden and cherished now bears her name. 'Margery Fish' is one of the most diminutive of the astrantias, with smaller umbels of flowers. The bracts are white, and the pink colour is concentrated in the "pins" supporting the tiny florets. I'm reminded of old-fashioned ladies' brooches, all silver set with clusters of garnets and pearls, and in need of polishing.

Astrantias form attractive clumps of lobed leaves. The height will vary according to the variety and culture, but they usually hit two feet or so (60cm). They are undemanding, thriving in sun or partial sun, but need a moist soil. Quick-draining sandy soil needs to be amended with organic matter to improve water retention. In areas of hot summers, midday shade is preferable. Astrantias increase by a running rootstock, although it should not be inferred that they are invasive, merely robust.

Astrantia is a member of the carrot family, the Umbelliferae, which also includes the charming Queen Anne's Lace, *Daucus carota*. There is a family resemblance, but while Queen Anne's Lace is the darling of arrangers, very few consider *Astrantia* as a cutting flower. Yet it is long-lasting in water, and imparts a lovely texture. Especially in a miniature bouquet the delicate structure of Hattie's Pincushion can best be appreciated.

This exotic species arrived in 1823 from China, yet has a universal quality of seeming at home at once and has been included in gardens halfway around the world from its original home. *Belamcanda* appears to be a modification of its eastern Asian name, while *chinensis* pinpoints its origin. The plant had uses in Oriental healing. Linnaeus originally classified it as *Ixia chinensis*, because of its resemblance to the bulbous plants from southern Africa now popular with florists as cut flowers.

Perhaps the sword-shaped leaves, so closely resembling its familiar iris kin, may fool the casual observer. There are slight differences: the foliage is a brighter green than the glaucous leaves of the bearded iris, and the stems are arranged zigzag fashion at the base of the stem. The real surprise comes when the clusters of thin buds unfurl into six-petalled blooms. The waxy flowers, more than an inch (2.5cm) across, are sandy yellow or pale orange with an overlay of reddish-orange spots. The pattern is not a fixed one, but appears like watercolours on a damp page. This led to its being called Leopard Flower.

Each flower lasts only a day, and twists itself up when spent, like a dishcloth wrung to squeeze it dry. Flowers are produced for many weeks in high summer, finally fading in late August or early September. The show doesn't end, for then, in the autumn, fat seedpods swell. As the leaves yellow and dry, the pods burst and curl back. Inside, bunches of black seeds stud the dry ribs.

It may sound patently obvious, but to

Belamcanda chinensis Iridaceae

BLACKBERRY LILY

ABOVE, flowers of *Belamcanda chinensis* display orange spots. Although each flower lasts but a single day, they are produced in great profusion, BELOW. The seedpods split in the autumn to reveal the shiny "blackberries," OPPOSITE.

enjoy the "blackberries" later—some gardeners even prefer the seeds to the flowers—it is necessary not to deadhead (to remove the spent flowers) earlier in the season. I learned this the first year I grew *Belamcanda*, when, like a good fussbudget, I absentmindedly and systematically performed my deeply ingrained daily ritual of deadheading. I deprived myself of the payoff. I did not make the same mistake

twice. The seed heads are delightful for winter arrangements, and will last for years (although it's best to start fresh each autumn, discarding the dried specimens and planting the seeds). It is easy to germinate the seeds in the greenhouse or under lights, and plant the young plants in the cutting garden or nursery bed. They will generally bloom the second year from a spring sowing.

There seems to be some confusion as to the hardiness of belamcandas. While they are steadfast with me even after winters with scathing thirty degrees below, they sometimes succumb in much milder areas. The cold is not the problem; rather, they need protection from excess moisture or they will rot. Well-drained sandy loam suits the rhizomes best, and situating them in raised beds or on slopes may be the key to survival in wetter places. Blackberry Lilies bloom best with at least a half day of sun, but leaf tips may singe in full sun, especially during dry spells. The thing to remember is that they need plenty of moisture during the growing season, but very little in the winter. The cautious gardener may wish to cover plants thoroughly with evergreen boughs, or the like, in colder areas.

Even though the flowering stems grow to three feet (90cm) or more, there's an advantage to planting a clump of *Belamcanda* near the front of a bed. The intricacies of the flowers and fruit can best be examined at close range. The iris-like foliage can be offset by the round leaves and delicate flower sprays of Coralbells, *Heuchera sanguinea*, at its feet. Brassy golden Gloriosa Daisies, *Rudbeckia hirta*, provide a brilliant backdrop.

Following this plant through history is an exercise in keeping up with name changes. It started its garden career as a giant member of the Saxifrage family. Later known as *Megasea*, it finally has its own genus of *Bergenia*. The name honours the German botanist Karl August von Bergen. The passage of *Bergenia* into gardens was through special hands. Linnaeus himself received the first one grown in gardens in 1760 from the empress of Russia. The species, *B. crassifolia*, and *B. cordifolia*, which arrived in England in 1779, were Siberian.

Since they are fair in flower and foliage, Alice Coats, an early advocate of the old-fashioned flowers, wondered why they hadn't received an affectionate name like that given to *Saxifraga × urbium*, London Pride. She suggested Liverpool Love or Leeds' Delight. She may have been un-aware, or did not think it suitable, that they had been dubbed Pigsqueaks. (By clasping one of the large leathery leaves between thumb and forefinger and strok-ing with the thumb, it is possible to elicit a swinelike grunt. This, of course, is not to everyone's taste, especially since to get the effect it helps to spit on one's fingers. After this garden party icebreaker, one may also set a match to a neighbouring Gas Plant, *Dictamnus albus*, achieving a flash of flame from its volatile oils, as well as an unparalleled reputation for horticultural high jinks.)

Aside from their entertaining qualities, bergenias work well as decorative plants. Showy heads of deep pink flowers bloom with the daffodils, but it is the foliage that

has earned it the gratitude of generations of gardeners. The bold, round leaves, often ten inches (25cm) across, are invaluable in the garden, and their uses are extensive. The shiny texture and shape of the clumps, growing to a foot and a half (45cm) tall, contrast well with so many other plants. In all but the harshest climates, the leaves are evergreen and assume mahogany-red tints in the autumn; they look best with a dusting of fresh snow.

The two most common species, B. cordifolia and B. crassifolia are so similar that some regard them as variants of the same species. The latter is distinguished by leaves that tend to remain green in colder months, and by the flower clusters, held on shorter stems, which have nodding flowers. Gardeners need not worry much about the differences, since their culture and uses are identical. In the wild, bergenias grow in forests, along streams, on rocky hills, and in alpine meadows; in short, bergenias can adapt to almost any situation a gardener can invent. Bergenias may be seen in their homelands of Siberia and Mongolia in vast numbers, with some patches covering several square miles.

An unusual silent species, B. ciliata was introduced in 1819 from Nepal. It differs

OPPOSITE, *Bergenia cordifolia* has colonized an island of a water lily pool. Pigsqueaks display flower clusters in spring, ABOVE, and leatherlike foliage throughout the year, BELOW.

from the Pigsqueaks in that the leaves are covered with fine hairs, something like those of an African violet. The margins are toothed, and the leaves are broader. The effect is silky and striking. The leaves don't live through the winter, but appear early with the slightly fragrant, pink-blushed flowers, which bloom earlier than those of other bergenias.

All three species are used in their native lands to make tea. A dye is extracted from the roots of B. ciliata; and B. crassifolia has been employed in the tanning process, and it is sometimes called Leatherleaf.

Bergenias thrive almost anywhere, in average soil and with little attention. Sunny beds are suitable if the soil doesn't dry out, but light shade is ideal, and they are particularly good for dry shade where hostas fail to thrive. They may be left to slowly establish large colonies, or they can easily be transplanted by division in the spring. They are long-lived, and tolerate city conditions. Gertrude Jekyll planted them frequently in perennial borders, but she used them elsewhere, too. In the paved courtyard next to her house, she filled Italian terra-cotta pots with many plants, some for flowers and some, like bergenias, for the texture (and perhaps the sound) of the leathery leaves.

Bergenia Saxifragaceae

Bergenia ciliata

Bergenia cordifolia

PIGSQUEAK

Joseph Breck of Boston described himself as a seedsman and florist. He both chronicled and helped to set gardening tastes. In *The Flower Garden* (1851) he wrote about the campanulas, "This is a large family of plants, mostly handsome, hardy, perennial; some of them are very beautiful, and about all suitable for ornamenting the borders. We have one indigenous species, which is very pretty, and worthy a place in the border; found abundantly on the banks of the Merrimack river, at and above Lowell. It is very much like *C. rotundifolia*, of England. Having cultivated them side by side, we can see but a shade's difference." It turned out the species were one and the same, and the Bluebells of Scotland are the same as the Harebells of America. Separated by global geological changes, ice ages, and time, the Harebell proved adaptable and tenacious.

The Bluebell was one of the first wildings to be invited into the garden for its beauty alone. It has been beloved by generations of poets. Emily Bronte wrote at her Yorkshire home in 1846:

"The Bluebell is the sweetest flower
That waves in summer air:
Its blossoms have the mightiest power
To soothe my spirit's care"

The Peach-leaved Bellflower, *C. persicifolia*, a native of central Europe and Asia, was grown in England as early as the sixteenth century. The elegant Spode-blue or white

Campanula carpatica

CARPATHIAN
HAREBELL

Campanula latiloba

Campanula persicifolia

PEACH-LEAVED
BELLFLOWER

Campanula
poscharskyana

CREEPING
BELLFLOWER

Campanula punctata

Campanula rotundifolia

HAREBELL

OPPOSITE, *C. rotundifolia* is paired with *Tanacetum densum* and *Asparagus densiflorus* 'Sprengeri'. Flowering *C. poscharkyana* contrasts with *Phlomis fruticosa*, ABOVE.

bells were almost superseded by double forms by the late 1700s, but now these are very rare themselves. The single forms need no improvement as far as I'm concerned. The nodding goblet-shaped bells dangle from three-foot (91cm) stems. The main flush of bloom is in June, but scattered flowers appear throughout the summer. Blue-flowered plants will often produce white offspring.

John Parkinson asserted that the distilled water made from the leaves and flowers was good for the skin and "maketh the face very splendent and clear." The water was also used as a gargle, and the young roots could be eaten, although Victorian garden writer Shirley Hibberd indicated that was only the case "in places where the natives are not particular about their salads and side-dishes."

The wild Rampion of Europe, *C. rapunculus*, figured in a fairy tale collected by the Brothers Grimm. In it, a husband raided the neighbouring witch's garden for the tender Rampion greens to satisfy the cravings of his wife. He was apprehended by the witch, who was very annoyed and absconded with their firstborn and locked her in a tower. The witch, besides being up on her Latin, had an ironic bent, and named the girl Rapunzel (after *C. rapunculus*). For those unfamiliar with the story, the only way to enter the tower was to climb up to the window on poor Rapunzel's hair. Like Samson, her strength was in her long tresses. There are some frightening goings-on, as is usual in the Brothers (Very) Grimm, before the happy

Campanula Campanulaceae

girl-gets-prince ending. At least now we all know what Rampion is, and not to filch it from a witch.

The rare *C. punctata* was introduced from Japan in 1813. In contrast to the traditional blue colour of many of the campanulas, this one has puffy tubular bells of cream, infused with pale rose. Inside, the bells are lightly spotted with mauve, somewhat like foxgloves. The leaves often take on a red autumn cast. The lovely flowers are nearly two inches (5cm) long—quite large considering the plant only grows a foot (30cm) high.

Another Asian species, this time from northern Turkey, arrived in 1828; *C. latiloba* (syn. *C. grandis*) is among the showiest of the bellflowers. In June, the stiff three-foot stems are clad for almost their entire length with wide starry blooms. A clump of the rich lavender-blue or white flowers is a fine sight. It seems unusual that all the flowers on a single stem could be open at one time. Some have included *C. latiloba* with *C. persicifolia*, resulting in some confusion, especially for gardeners. They

are two distinct species, as recognized in *The Flora of Turkey*. They need never be confused again.

The species of *Campanula* number in the hundreds, so it isn't surprising that the upright sorts have lower, sprawling counterparts. One of the first to be grown in gardens was *C. carpatica*, imported to England just before the start of the American Revolution. Its name declares its origin in the Carpathian Mountains of present-day Czechoslovakia and Poland, although it is sometimes called the Turkish Bellflower. The spreading mounds, less than a foot (30cm) tall, are covered with the blue bells, so typical of the genus, during a great part of the summer. They are invaluable plants for the front of beds and sunny banks.

Campanula persicifolia possesses timeless appeal planted with the sulphur-green *Cushion Spurge*, *Euphorbia seguierana*, BELOW LEFT. The stems of *C. latiloba* are studded with flowers, BELOW RIGHT. Creeping Bellflower, *C. poscharskyana*, softens stonework, OPPOSITE.

The pretty Creeping Bellflower, *C. poscharskyana*, arrived in gardens just over a hundred years ago from Yugoslavia. Seeing it tumble over rocks and colonize pathways, it's hard to believe it hasn't always been a feature of the English garden. The mounds of tiny leaves are rich lavender-blue in early summer. This, like most of the campanulas, can take care of itself, and must be given free rein to spread.

Bellflowers are never stingy with their flowers, and it takes little to coax a lavish display from them. Most prefer partly sunny situations and adequate water, as do border plants such as columbines and daisies. Hardy almost everywhere, they are not prone to disease or pests. Best of all, the many sorts impart a feeling of old-world grace to any garden. The taller species are classic components of the perennial border; there is hardly a better companion for plump Cabbage Roses or show-stopping peonies. There is no pretention about the bellflowers; the utter lack of it is what has endeared them to poets and gardeners alike.

Technically speaking, *Campsis radicans* is a vine, but its spectacular floral display—such an integral part of a summer garden—is so characteristically old-fashioned as to warrant its inclusion here. As hedges of lilacs epitomize May, so the Trumpet Vine, in blazing scarlet splendour, symbolizes midsummer. It is a quintessential feature of old Victorian houses of the American Midwest. Clambering up pergolas, poles, and rough walls, Trumpet Vines cloak old gardens with wild abandon. This is hardly surprising, as the plant is native to many states of mid-America, and ranges from Illinois, Ohio, and New Jersey south to Florida and as far west as Texas. It is found growing in the wild at the outskirts of woodlands, especially on dead trees or along the ground if no support is available. When settlers first came to the continent, the species was not especially common; as forests were cleared, the sun-loving *Campsis* benefitted, and is now found growing in hedgerows and on roadside fences. It has further extended its range by escaping from gardens in some areas. (I have always enjoyed the image of a plant sneaking stealthily over the fence at midnight, free at last, and planting itself in the wild.)

John Tradescant Junior is credited with the discovery of Trumpet Vine during a visit to the Virginia colony in 1637. The name is from the Greek *kampsis*, meaning "turning," alluding to the four curved stamens of the flowers. The specific epithet of its name, *radicans*, refers to the clinging aerial rootlets. The vine, also called

Trumpet Creeper and Cow-itch, is classified as a member of the family Bignoniaceae, and was formerly known as *Bignonia*, and before that as *Tecoma*, under which name it was introduced to English gardeners just a few years after Tradescant's visit.

After visiting an Indian village of the Nottoway tribe, Colonel William Byrd, a Virginia plantation owner, wrote in 1728 of an Indian princess who "poisoned herself like an Old Roman with the root of the trumpet plant." We can be fairly sure that his comparison refers only to the manner of her death, not its cause, which would have been unknown in ancient Rome. Aside from some possible inconvenience to cattle, the Trumpet Vine is not regarded as a dangerous plant, although it clearly should not be ingested.

The funnel-shaped flowers, each about three inches (8cm) long, are held in tight clusters. As many as eight or ten flowers may bloom simultaneously in each cluster. The scarlet colour is especially vivid on the lip of the trumpet, which splits into five recurving segments, while the throat is more melon-coloured. The colour intensity varies a little from orange to red; the variety 'Flava' is a cream-yellow variant. The main display is in July and August, but occasional flowers may appear into autumn. The vines can grow to thirty feet (9m), clinging to supports with aerial roots. The compound leaves, deep green and shiny, commonly have nine to eleven leaflets.

The only other species, *C. grandiflora* from China and Japan, climbs less vigorously. In America, it is most suited to mild-winter areas such as Oregon, although it is hardy as far north as Boston, and its similarly toned flowers are more cup-shaped. It blooms in July and August.

Planting a Trumpet Vine is an investment in the future, for it will live for many generations. The site, like that for the long-lived peony, should be considered carefully before planting, and fertile, well-drained soil provided. It thrives in a sunny situation. Trumpet Vines need enough room to scamper up a wall or fence; they are generally unsuitable for wooden structures because of the difficulties involved when painting. Pinch back the growing tips of new plants to encourage branching near the base. They may need initial support before the aerial roots, with which they fasten themselves, develop. Several years are necessary before blossoms are produced, and several more before full glory is achieved. Trumpet Vines are remarkably self-sufficient, and have few

serious disease or insect problems. Root division can be done successfully in the spring, or cuttings can be rooted. Pruning, if desired, should be done in late winter before new growth begins. Where no support is available, gardeners can prune plants to make bushes or hedges.

Children of the Midwest (and perhaps other places) have been known to select plump buds, ready to open, sneak up behind an unsuspecting victim, and pop them on the person's head. This makes a reasonably effective and startling bang. The opened flowers are favourites of bees and hummingbirds. The plant is not quite universally admired. I once saw a particularly floriferous specimen scrambling over the front fence of a house and I told the owner, sitting on his front porch, how pretty it looked. He offered me a shovel if I would haul it away—it attracted too many bees to suit him.

Campsis radicans Bignoniaceae

TRUMPET VINE

A stoic marble lion, OPPOSITE, is crowned by a temporary wreath of the tubular flowers of Trumpet Vine, *Campsis radicans*, which last for days after cutting. A handsome specimen of Trumpet Vine in full fiery bloom during late July graces a Midwestern house of late Victorian vintage, ABOVE, where it is trained as an upright hedge rather than as a climber.

Centranthus ruber Valerianaceae

JUPITER'S BEARD

Centranthus ruber, commonly known as Jupiter's Beard, has grown for so long in England that the circumstances of its introduction are obscured by time. It is possible the Romans may have brought this native of the Mediterranean region with them, either purposely or by chance seeds. The name, sometimes called *Kentranthus*, is derived from the Greek *kentron*, a spur, and *anthos*, a flower, and alludes to the small spurs at the base of the small flower. It is a member of the valerian family.

Gerard wrote, "It groweth plentifully in my garden, being a great ornament to the same, and not common in England." It naturalized itself in many areas quickly though, especially in southern England and Ireland. It acquired many folk names on its journeys, including Red Spur, Bovisand Soldier, Good Neighbourhood, and Setwall. The last is singularly appropriate, as it became a picturesque wall plant and as William Hanbury, a gardening clergyman, noted in 1770, it "will come up in the crevices of old walls and buildings; so that they are often industriously put between the stones of ruins, grottos, etc.; which growing, flower strong, and have a good effect most part of the summer." Its southern European roots serve it well; once introduced, *Centranthus* survives in seemingly impossible conditions. I remember seeing a stone wall, perhaps twelve feet (3.6m) high and nearly two hundred feet (61m) long, in a village near Chipping Campden, in the Cotswolds. Great billows of scarlet, coral, and white *Centranthus* nearly obscured the wall.

Jupiter's Beard, *Centranthus ruber*, OPPOSITE, blooms with the rose 'Parkdirektor Riggers'. ABOVE, *C. ruber* grows in old rockwork. ILLUSTRATION, TOP, *Valeriana officinalis*.

The first white seedling was reported by a gardener in Essex in 1604, and a deep copper-red variety, 'Atrococcineus,' is striking. Seedlings are apt to display diversity, and white is not uncommon. *Centranthus* can be a prodigious seeder if the spent heads aren't removed, although they tend to place themselves in such an artistic fashion that the young plants are nearly always welcome. Plants are not long-lived anyway—five years seems to be realistic—so it is best to have young plants coming along. As might be guessed from their cliff-hanging habits, well-drained soil and sun suit them well, although they are adaptable to more mundane locations, such as the flower bed. Jupiter's Beard has a long flowering season, and the rounded airy heads grow to two or three feet (61-120cm) in height. The striking colour, probably best described as deep coral pink, should be segregated from rosy red and magenta flowers, but harmonizes with the tea rose 'Peace,' whose corn silk petals are blushed with coral. The pure white blooms of *Lychnis coronaria* 'Alba,' a form of the common Rose Campion, intensify the coral colouration of *Centranthus*, and the Campion's grey foliage complements the glaucous leaves.

Centranthus has no healing properties, although the leaves were eaten in Sicily and southern Italy. The seeds, however, were employed in the embalming practice very long ago, and some that were removed from a twelfth-century cerecloth are reported to have been germinated by curious nineteenth-century botanists.

The medicinal plant of this family is Valerian, *Valeriana officinalis*. Called Heal All and Capon's Tail (from a fancied resemblance to hen feathers), it grew in England as early as the sixteenth century, after being introduced from central Europe. The genus name stems from the Latin word *valere*, meaning "to be strong, healthy." Heal All tea was prescribed for a case of nerves. Juice squeezed from the roots was used to treat those afflicted with St. Vitus' dance or epilepsy. Thomas Jefferson wrote of its medicinal virtues. Valerian tea calmed the nerves after air raids during the First World War.

The root was found to have an intoxicating effect on cats, making them even more delirious than Catmint. It is said that a small piece thrown to a lion will cause him to roll around with it excitedly. It has been suggested that the magic of the Pied Piper of Hamlin was not in his flute but in his pocket; rats are as ecstatic as cats over the fabled roots. I have grown Valerian for many years, delighting in the sweet vanilla-smelling pink flowers borne in sprays in late May. The neighbourhood cats have never taken notice of the plants, and I assume they take care of any rodents that might.

Species of *Clematis* are found in temperate areas throughout the world. The name comes from the Greek word *klema*, and *klematis* was Dioscorides' name for a vine with slender branches. In medieval times, beggars would rub the sap into small cuts to produce frightening, yet superficial, sores that would elicit more generous alms. The roots were dried and used as shampoos, and Indians used the bark to treat fevers.

There is some confusion about the pronunciation of the name. Either clem-uh-tis, with the accent on the first syllable, or clem-a-tis, with the accent on the second syllable and with a flat *a*, is acceptable. The first has a slight edge. I've also heard several other interpretations—climb-at-us may suggest a rampaging vine: it is not correct.

The typical *Clematis* is usually pictured as a large-flowered climber, but the genus is varied. The upright, or bush, types have been grown in perennial borders for many years. The non-vining *Clematis* dies to the ground each winter. Gerard distinguished these types from the vines, commenting that the one he grew "dieth at the approch of winter, and recovereth againe from the roote, which endureth."

Like the vining species, the nonvining ones can be separated into those with bell-shaped flowers, and those with wide-spreading petals. Foremost among the former is *C. integrifolia*. The specific epithet refers to the thin, undivided leaves, although gardeners are far more interested in the violet-blue flowers. The pendant four-petalled blooms dangle gracefully from plants growing to over two feet (60cm). In its native southern European environs the plant is inclined to sprawl, so it is advantageous to provide a framework of brush and twigs, through which the stems thread themselves for support. The two-inch (5cm) flowers, with a parchment-coloured centre, recurve delicately. Parkinson described the petals as "standing like a crosse . . . of a faire blew or skie colour, with a thicke pale yellow short thrumme, made like a head in the middle." They are followed by a tangle of plumed seed heads. The entire plant has a downy appearance owing to a coat of fine hairs.

C. integrifolia has been grown in English gardens since 1573. The Tradescants called it "the greater Hungarian Climer, with blew flower." Joseph Breck grew it in

Boston as early as 1850, and admired the plant for "producing nodding, bell-shaped, blue flowers, most of the season."

Native to China, a variety at first called *Clematis davidiana* was discovered in 1867 by Abbé Armand David, the French missionary whose journeys led him to remote parts of Inner Mongolia. It is now represented as *C. heracleifolia*. The Latin name refers to the resemblance of the leaves to those of the Cow Parsnip, *Heracleum*. The plants, which are sometimes woody at the base, grow to three feet (90cm) or more. The toothed leaves, grouped in sets of three, are topped in late summer with clusters of fragrant pale blue flowers resembling hyacinths. The individual flowers, about one inch long, have four recurving sepals, or petals. The variety *davidiana*, found by Père David, is characterized by its Wedgwood-blue colour.

Clematis recta differs from the other two by its up-facing, open-petalled flowers. This native of France and Germany was introduced in 1573. The white flowers grow in large panicles on stems that usually reach a height of three feet (90cm), but in rich soil can attain six feet (120cm). Gertrude Jekyll characterized the flower's colour as "foam-white," and liked to pair it with blue delphiniums. The blossoms are sweet-smelling, and were formerly grown on a large scale for the cut-flower trade, but lamentably have fallen from the florists' favour. A rare double form was recorded by 1860, and a variety with a purple cast to the foliage was known as early as 1772. The flowers are followed by silvery puffs of seeds.

For all their charm, and high praise from gardeners in the past, the shrub clematises are seldom seen in gardens. While the climbing species and hybrids enjoy widespread popularity, the upright types languish in obscurity. In the garden, all-blue themes can easily incorporate *C. integrifolia* and *C. heracleifolia* var. *davidiana*. The blue bells also look pretty with daylilies, roses, and veronicas. They are hardy almost everywhere, and benefit from sunny positions. Like the rest of the genus, they require an alkaline soil, meaning that a gardener with acidic soil should apply lime. Clematis may be grown from cuttings or seeds, although both means require a degree of technical skill. Seeds often need a period of freezing temperatures to break dormancy. Seedlings should be carefully protected during their first winter.

Clematis
Ranunculaceae

Clematis heracleifolia DAVID'S CLEMATIS

Clematis integrifolia BUSH CLEMATIS

Clematis recta UPRIGHT CLEMATIS

The nodding violet blossoms of *Clematis integrifolia*, LEFT, are displayed on upright stems, although some support is usually needed. *Clematis heracleifolia* 'Davidiana' bears fragrant flowers in clusters, ILLUSTRATION, OPPOSITE.

Crucianella stylosa came to gardens in 1836 from the area now called Iran. It is a member of Rubiaceae, the madder family, which also boasts such wildly divergent plants as gardenia, coffee, and the tree from which quinine is extracted. The Latin name comes from *crucis*, and means little cross, while *stylosa* refers to the prominent styles, the filaments protruding from the flowers. Though it has a common name—Crosswort—it is not a common plant. Perhaps it has been held back by an utterly forgettable old name; it was formerly labelled *Phuopsis stylosa*.

The modern garden hosts flowers from the far corners of the globe. The garden is a melting pot where green immigrants are swiftly assimilated. Even so, most gardeners would be hard pressed to name a plant growing in their gardens that came from Iran. Perhaps Crosswort blends in so well because the flower heads look like small versions of *Centranthus*, the well-known Jupiter's Beard. Even the colour, a paler shade of coral pink, is reminiscent of Jupiter's Beard. (The old name *Phuopsis* alludes to its similarity to *Valeriana phu*, a close relative of *Centranthus*.)

Crosswort grows from eight to twelve inches (20-30cm) high in mat-forming mounds. The stems are covered with whorls of short, thin leaves. Each stem is crowned with a round head of flowers in June, which continue to bloom throughout most of the summer. The tiny star-shaped flowers are packed in tight clusters. The scent is very slight, although after a rain it is more perceptible. It is difficult to liken

the smell to anything else, although some have suggested goats. This is rather unkind, and should not deter the picking of flowers for informal arrangements, for they are long-lasting and one has to absolutely bury the nose in them to detect anything.

Crosswort's value lies not in its own

beauty, which is considerable but not startling, but rather in its ability to unify and highlight other, showier flowers. Its tone is rather more sharp than the pinks of dianthuses or mallows. It is striking in contrast with deep purple flowers. The flowers can be planted as edgings or

Crucianella stylosa
Rubiaceae

CROSSWORT

at the fronts of perennial beds to soften the transition to the pavement. In these days of no-fuss groundcovers, Crosswort performs admirably in the role. It thrives in rock gardens, giving colour in summer after the jewels of spring have finished.

Although it has never been grown

C. stylosa and *Leontopodium alpinum* spill from a birdhouse, OPPOSITE. BELOW, *C. stylosa* enlivens a perennial border, and its sharp pink colour is splendid with *Lavandula angustifolia*, *Alchemilla mollis*, and *Salvia superba*. ILLUSTRATION, OPPOSITE, the prominent styles give the species its name.

extensively, Crosswort has no special requirements. It adapts to almost any soil in part shade or sun, with average water. It is not troubled by insects or diseases. The mats of foliage will spread slowly to several feet, and new plants may be obtained from seed, cuttings, or division.

Erigeron Compositae

Erigeron is a genus of daisylike flowers found growing throughout the world. The Latin name is puzzling, being derived from the Greek words *eri*, "early," and *geron*, "old man." Early old man? Perhaps this can be explained by the early development of the fluffy seed heads of some kinds, the white-bearded seeds (in need of Grecian formula) suggesting premature old age. Another, more plausible explanation may be that *er* is also a form of the Greek word for spring, and "old-man-in-spring" would allude to the downy covering of the foliage early in the season. The common name "Fleabane" is more easily explained, since the native British species, *E. acris* was gathered and burned, the acrid smoke driving fleas from dwellings. One of the North American fleabanes, *E. annuus*, is a naturalized wildflower in Europe and England. Its seeds were accidentally transported during an ocean voyage inside a stuffed bird.

The flowers of the fleabanes have yellow centres, and very narrow petals, properly called ray-florets. They are closely related to the perennial asters, known as Michaelmas daisies. The asters usually have a single row of ray-florets, as opposed to the double rows of the fleabanes, which do not wait to bloom until the feast day of St. Michael, September 29.

The showiest of the fleabanes, *E. speciosus*, was discovered near Fort Vancouver by David Douglas, and debuted as a garden flower in 1826. The flowers are pale rosy lavender, although selected forms may display a richer hue. They are

LEFT, the flowers of a selection of *E. speciosus*, bloom in June in a rock garden. ABOVE, *E. speciosus* spills onto a pathway. BELOW, *E. karvinskianus* seeded in stonework.

Erigeron karvinskianus
MEXICAN FLEABANE

Erigeron speciosus
FLEABANE

clustered on the stems and grow to two feet (60cm) with an equal spread. *E. formosissimus*, native to the Rocky Mountains and the Black Hills, is similar but shorter, and its posture is more relaxed.

Dainty *E. karvinskianus* (syn. *E. mucronatus*) is a perennial species native to Mexico and Panama that has demonstrated a surprising adaptability to colder climates. The species was named for Baron von Karwinski of Munich, who travelled extensively in Central America in the mid 1800s. It might be classified as a charming weed with the ability to bloom nonstop all summer. Each solitary flower is less than an inch (2.5cm) across and opens on a nine-inch (23cm) stem; the flower rays open white, turn pink, and finally fade to wine-red. It sows itself in walls and cracks between stones. Christopher Lloyd, whose garden at Great Dixter in East Sussex abounds with the tiny Mexican Fleabane, writes of its easy care, "We cut the old growth back in early spring to neaten it up and away it goes, white daisies changing to pink as they age. It is in every wall, step riser and paving crack untreated with weedkiller. A charmer until late in the year when it becomes untidy again." Though some are so uncharitable as to characterize it as invasive, we should consider ourselves lucky to be so invaded.

Fleabanes are of the easiest culture, needing only ordinary soil of reasonable fertility, with moderate water, since they are intolerant of soggy muck. They are ideal for east-facing exposures, since they succeed best with protection from the midday sun, but too much shade will inhibit flowering and encourage floppy stems. The showy fleabanes are hardy in northern gardens, and the Mexican Fleabane is variable, but since it blooms the first year from seed, there is little reason to discriminate against it on grounds of hardiness.

Eryngium is a fascinating, albeit confused, genus of flowers, many of which are useful in the garden, for arranging, and for drying. There is a tangle of species and hybrids, but all have thistle-like flowers, some esteemed for unusual metallic sheens. The English Wild Sea Holly, *E. maritimum*, has been valued since Anglo-Saxon times. The roots of this "thystle of the sea," or "yringe," were reputed to cure a multitude of ills, including serpent bites, broken bones, thorns in the flesh, and "imposthumes" (abscesses) in the ear. Culpeper, trying his hand at chiropractic, prescribed the roots "for those that have their necks drawn awry, and cannot turn them without turning their whole body." The roots were candied and had supposed aphrodisiac properties. Falstaff, in *The Merry Wives of Windsor*, mentions "eringoes," likening them to "kissing comfits," a comfit being a candied sweetmeat. Gerard advocated the sweets for "people that no delight or appetite to venerie, nourishing and restoring the aged and amending defects of nature in the younger."

The town of Colchester, Essex, was famous for its eryngoes as early as 1650, and they were produced there until the beginning of the nineteenth century. At one point, Sea Holly root was the key ingredient in a concoction known as mock asses' milk (which also contained garden snails) that was used to feed babies and consumptives, who most likely were too weak to protest.

The Wild Sea Holly is rarely seen in gardens, although its steel-blue flowers and

Eryngium
Umbelliferae

Eryngium giganteum GIANT SEA HOLLY

Eryngium maritimum WILD SEA HOLLY

Eryngium planum SEA HOLLY

A Busby Berkeley view of *Eryngium giganteum*, OPPOSITE, reveals its symmetry. ILLUSTRATION, TOP, *E. maritimum*. ABOVE, *Eryngium giganteum* sparkles when paired with blue *Anchusa azurea* and daisies. *E. planum* and silver *Santolina chamaecyparissus* enhance vibrant Cockscomb and Cosmos, BELOW.

ABOVE, sprays of the small steely blue cones of *Eryngium planum* add texture to an informal arrangement of Goldenrod, *Solidago canadensis*, and white pompoms of *Hydrangea arborescens* 'Annabelle'. A hybrid form of *Eryngium alpinum* is carefully positioned at the junction of two paths, OPPOSITE, to invite closer inspection of the frilled calyx of each flower.

grey leaves would certainly merit its inclusion. The thick leaves are an adaptation to prevent water loss and protect the plant from sea spray. It is not nearly as common as in the past; generations of beachgoers have systematically uprooted it to avoid the pain of barefoot contact with the spiny leaves. Growing to only a foot (30cm), it has probably been overshadowed by taller species.

E. alpinum, from mountainous Europe, was grown as early as 1597. Its teasel-like blue cones are surrounded by frilled prickly segments of the calyx. *E. planum* arrived about the same time from eastern Europe. The whole plant is suffused with a blue-green tint, and the clusters of small flowers are highly valued for cutting. Both species grow to three feet (90cm).

The most imposing sea holly is the aptly named *E. giganteum* from Iran and the Caucasus Mountains. The large flowers, of seafoam green or grey-blue, have a silver sheen, and are arranged in symmetrical

clusters of ruffled calyx bracts. It is sometimes called Miss Willmott's Ghost, after the famous nineteenth-century plantswoman Ellen Willmott. From stashes of seeds concealed in her pockets, she would nonchalantly sprinkle seeds where she deemed necessary in gardens she visited. The Giant Sea Holly grows on stiff stems to three feet (90cm), and is short-lived, often monocarpic, meaning it dies after blooming, although it seeds itself liberally and grows quickly.

E. × oliveranum is a very old hybrid grown as early as 1730, later a favourite of Gertrude Jekyll. Its parentage is uncertain, although it probably involves *E. alpinum*. William Robinson was justifiably extravagant in his praise, saying, "The stems are so singularly beautiful with their vivid steel-blue tints . . . with the involucre [bracts at the base of the flower] even more brilliant, that the effect is hardly excelled." It is the rare plant that commands attention for its lovely stems. The

finely serrated leaves, resembling those of cut-leaf maples, have an olive-green cast, underscoring the lacy blue collars of the flower cones.

To gardeners accustomed to bright dahlias and petunias, it may be a challenge to picture the Sea Holly in their garden. As a plant of distinction and subtlety, it should be positioned carefully, since the flowers can be lost if set too far back in a planting. Imagine the flowers, glinting in the light, placed in front of a mass of Baby's Breath or Sea Kale. All sorts of white flowers benefit from companionship with sea hollies, like lilies, or daisies. It is especially pretty with the pale pink clusters of the little rose called 'The Fairy,' and also may be used to effect with stronger colours like crimson, orange, or magenta.

Sea hollies thrive in open, sunny gardens in well-drained soils, although they are remarkably tolerant of poor, stony ground. They are considered hardy almost everywhere except where roots may rot from excessive moisture. They bloom in June and July, and dry well if cut early.

Gardening goatherds may also find a practical use for the flowers, beyond their beauty in the border. The ancient Greeks, according to Gerard, discovered (no one knows how or why) that if a flower were given to one goat in a flock, "it causeth her first to stand still, and afterwards the whole flock, till such time as the sheepherd take it from her mouth." The derivation of the name (which unfortunately does not mean "goat still" but, surprisingly, is translated by some as "goat's beard") is from the Greek *eryngion*, and is explained as a plant used to cure indigestion and wind.

The word "gentian" brings images to our minds of the vivid blue alpine trumpets, and a flower of yellow colouration never enters the picture. Nevertheless, the Golden Gentian, *Gentiana lutea*, was among the first of the genus to find favour in the garden. In tradition, Gentius, King of Illyria (part of present-day Yugoslavia) first discovered the medicinal powers of its root in about 500 B.C., and the plant bears his name. In truth, the ancient Egyptians employed the Golden Gentian a thousand years before; prescriptions inscribed on papyrus have been found buried with a mummy at Thebes. This suggests the patient did not respond as hoped to the tonic bitters, but the gentian has been a valued and effective healing plant through-out history.

It was first introduced in England by Gerard, who received it from an apothe-cary friend on the Continent about 1600. Everybody jumped on the bandwagon. Parkinson was convinced it would un-doubtedly work wondrous cures, if it were not despised for the bitter flavour "by reason of our daintie tastes." It was added to beer before hops were imported to impart the characteristic flavour. Not surprisingly, it was called Bitterwort. Other folknames were the inexplicable Bald-money, and Felwort—popularly associated with its ability to cure felons, now called galls. (Would that latter-day felons, who may have a lot of gall, were so easily treated!) Culpeper, always out in left field, claimed the gentian was under the domin-ion of Mars, and confidently claimed, "when kine are bitten in the udder by any venomous beast, do but stroke the place with the decoction . . . and it will instantly heal them."

Modern gardeners, who may or may not keep cattle or make beer, value the Golden Gentian to grace their June garden. The four-foot (120cm) flower stalks grow from impressive rosettes of crinkled glossy leaves. The clusters of yellow flowers are arranged in whorls. Tiers of the starry flowers, each with a prominent olive-green pistil, are cupped in large green bracts. From a distance, the combination of the yellow flowers and green bracts makes the whole look golden; the thin buds are gold too. The imposing flower stems, with their architectural quality, serve as luminous punctuation marks in the border. After the flowers have faded, the seed heads can be dried.

Although the gentians have a reputation as temperamental, *G. lutea* is not that difficult to grow. The soil should be fertile and the site sunny. It is propagated by seed, and the utmost care should be taken not to damage the root in transplanting. Good drainage is necessary, especially in winter, and the plants are tolerant of all but the most frigid winters. A straw mulch or covering of evergreen boughs may help to protect the crowns in winter. Success is by no means guaranteed. In the floral language of the Victorians, the Golden Gentian symbolized ingratitude, since "it so frequently dies under the culture of the gardener."

G. lutea is still grown commercially. The roots, which are shaped like turnips and weigh up to twenty-five pounds (11.5kg), are dug in autumn, dried, and made into gentian bitters, which improves the ap-petite and stimulates gastric activity. A recipe for the "elixir of life" calls for rhubarb, aloe, acorus, and Golden Gentian. It is said that chewing the root will discourage smokers; it would very likely discourage anybody.

GOLDEN GENTIAN

Three-foot stems of *G. lutea*, ABOVE, are surrounded by a sea of spode-blue blooms of the Peach-leaved Bellflower, *Campanula persicifolia*. OPPOSITE, the star-shaped flowers of *G. lutea* are held in leafy bracts arranged at intervals along the stem; below ground lie the massive roots that, when dried, are made into Gentian bitters.

Gentiana lutea Gentianaceae

 *Geranium* is a rich and varied genus of hardy perennials. They should not be confused with their distant cousins that decorate windowsills and parks during the summer, and are properly known as pelargoniums. At some point the bedding plants usurped the name in the vernacular, and it is unlikely they will ever relinquish it. To avoid any further confusion, the true geraniums are commonly called cranesbills, for their long thin seedpods.

Many of the cultivated species are native to England, or were introduced very early from the Continent or America. The native *G. pratense* was known to Gerard as Crowfoot Crane's-bill or *Gratia Dei* ("gift of God"), a common Old English name that stemmed from the German name *Gottesgnade*. This, in turn, came from the older "Odin's Grace," named for the supreme deity of Norse mythology. (Odin, or Woden, was the god of art and culture, not to mention of war and the dead.) The Normans called them Bassinets, from an Old French word meaning bowl-shaped flower. Romantic country folk knew them as Loving Andrews.

In Iceland, a blue-grey dye was extracted from the flowers and was considered "fittest for fighting men." The secret of making this precursor to navy blue has unfortunately been lost. Tradescant brought back the purple-blue–flowered *G.*

The magenta flowers of *G. psilostemon* are elegant against wild indigo and hybrid delphiniums, FAR LEFT. *G. pratense*, ILLUSTRATION, TOP, yields a lush border planting, LEFT, while *G. endressii* naturalizes itself in an informal cottage garden, ABOVE.

Geranium Geraniaceae

Geranium endressii

Geranium maculatum WOOD GERANIUM

Geranium pratense LOVING ANDREWS

Geranium psilostemon
ARMENIAN CRANESBILL

Geranium sanguineum BLOODY CRANESBILL

pratense from Archangel, a Russian seaport on the White Sea—he did not realize it also grew in northern parts of Britain—and it is probably this plant, which he called *Geranium flore serulle*, from which the dye was made. The flowers of a novel form of this species, 'Striatum,' are stippled with streaks and flecks of pale plum on a pearl background. Both Gerard and Parkinson grew this rare striped variety, thereafter called Queen Anne's Needlework. It should not be confused with the pretty wildflower Queen Anne's Lace, *Daucus carota*, and we should be grateful the queen didn't crochet or knit or darn for fear of sorting out the names.

The handsome native *G. sanguineum* was called Bloody Cranesbill, not for its flowers, which are a startling deep pink, but for its use as a wound-herb. The classically oriented Turner was cautious about this, stating, "The later writers have found that these kindes of Geranium are good for woundes and for other things that Dioscorides maketh no mention of . . . I dowt whether they have suche properties. . . ."

The hardy geraniums were favourites of William Robinson, who loathed the Victorians' annual bedding displays using the "other" geraniums. Their greatest charm lies in the simplicity of the blossoms, and the profusion with which they are produced. Arthur Johnson, a gardener from North Wales, marvelled at this latter quality, saying, "They fit into their surroundings with that subtle sympathy which weds the harebell to the heaths."

Lovely flowers, good foliage, and a willing disposition—some say too willing—recommend them to modern gardeners as well. These old flowers fit readily into the modern concept of groundcovers. The most vigorous kinds are weed-suppressing colonizers that may be given full rein to carpet large areas. There are many to choose from; with careful selection, gardeners may succeed in having varieties blooming throughout the season. All grow easily in sun or part sun with little attention, although they prefer not to be incinerated. In gardens where hot summers bake the beds, adequate water must be supplied.

G. macrorrhizum came from the south of Europe in 1576. In late spring, the pale pink flowers contrast with the five lobed aromatic leaves. It is reliable and vigorous as a trouble-free weed suppressor. The autumn foliage often turns red. Clumps grow a foot (30cm) high and spread two feet (60cm). The American species *G. maculatum* first graced English gardens in 1732. The two-foot mounds of divided leaves of the Wood Geranium are topped with clear lilac blossoms. Graham Stuart Thomas notes that it is "usually in flower in May, at which time there are few herbaceous plants to rival it, but it would be acclaimed at any time."

Victorian plant hunters found lovely *Geranium himalayense* growing in northern India. Like most of the cranesbills, the plant, RIGHT, forms dense hummocks which erupt into bloom in early summer, and the daintily-cut leaves turn red in the autumn, extending its usefulness in a border or as a ground cover planting.

The Pyrenees Mountains yielded the treasure of *G. endressii* in 1812. Gardeners rejoice in its long season of bloom. The silvery pink flowers, lightly etched with red, are complemented by light green buttercup-like leaves that are evergreen in milder regions. The dense two-foot (60cm) hummocks grow to about eighteen inches (45cm). The flowers of the cultivar 'Wargrave Pink' are tinted with salmon. Arthur Johnson found that ". . . they are vigorous colonizers and possessed of such admirable courage that with us they grow anywhere, in sun or shade, in grass or border, or bed of nettles."

Another mountain beauty, *G. himalayense*, arrived from Sikkim, in northern India, around 1880. The violet-blue flowers are delicately veined and appear in early summer. The finely cut leaves form foot-tall mounds, which make them suitable for a position near the edge of a bed.

Among the most spectacular of the cranesbills, *G. psilostemon* (the *p* is silent) was imported from Armenia in 1874. It is a plant of distinction, growing to four feet (120cm) with an equal spread. It is handsome in all respects. Brilliant magenta blooms, accented by the black centres, cover the clumps in June. The flower petals are traced with delicate, dark veins. Some people crinkle their noses at the mere mention of the colour magenta, but the joyfully rich-hued flowers of the Armenian Cranesbill are surprisingly elegant when paired with deep blue or purple. Its broad divided leaves are crimson-tinted in the autumn. It may be worth some extra effort, as it performs best in deeply dug loam, and a support of brush may help to keep it upright in the wind.

All things tropical were of great interest to gardeners and collectors of the nineteenth century. The giant Amazonian Water Lily, named *Victoria regia* (now *Victoria amazonica*) in honour of the queen, was discovered in 1837. With leaves six feet (1.8m) in diameter and capable of supporting a man (or at least a sunbonneted child, as Victorian portfolios always illustrate it), it was a great sensation when it was shown at the Crystal Palace at the opening of the Great Exhibition in 1851.

It should come as no surprise, then, that *Gunnera manicata* would hold the same fascination in the flower bed. The Giant Umbrella Leaf arrived in 1867 from Brazil, although a smaller but similar species, *G. chilensis*, had already whetted the gardening public's appetite since its 1840 debut. The American Peter Henderson had been impressed, and told of the "rhubarb-like leaves, which are fully three feet [90cm] across, born on thorny stems," and the size of the plant, with "a good specimen being from four to five feet [1.2–1.5m] high, and eight to ten feet [2.4–3m] in diameter, and forming an excellent subject for the sub-tropical garden."

Just around the corner, little more than twenty-five years later, loomed the Brazilian species, with leaves spreading up to and over six feet (1.8m) in length and bizarre flower cones—an unparalleled foliage plant, then and now. The leaves are the largest that can be grown in the temperate world. Graham Stuart Thomas observed, "One would hardly need to pick these—either the leaf or flower—unless one were decorating the Albert Hall."

Imagine growing the Umbrella Leaf for the first time. Assuming you have provided enough room for it at a marshy position near the water's edge, the crown, covered in brown hair, stirs to life in April. Prickly stalks grow quickly, unfurling vast pleated leaves. The puckered leaves are lobed and bristly. Light shining through them reveals an intricate network of supporting veins. In June, spiked clubs of dull green emerge from the interior of the tropical foliage, elongating like the cones of fir trees. One would not consider these flowers, but more like fruiting knobs. They are strange and wonderful, like some kind of flora out of prehistoric days.

The grande dame of garden artistry, Gertrude Jekyll, affirmed, "It was a good day for our water margins when the Giant Gunneras were introduced; for the immense size and noble form of their foliage enables us to make water-pictures on a scale that before was impossible. The

Gunnera
Gunneraceae

Gunnera chilensis UMBRELLA LEAF

Gunnera manicata GIANT UMBRELLA LEAF

Jagged, deeply-veined leaves, BELOW LEFT, rise from the crown of *Gunnera chilensis* in late spring. A quaint boathouse is secluded among *Rhododendron* and the reedy foliage of *Iris pseudacorus*, and framed by the massive leaves of gunnera, BELOW RIGHT.

Gunneras are so overpoweringly large that they dwarf everything near them; their size seems to demand some association with primeval rock-form and evidence of primeval force."

The Chilean Umbrella Leaf will grow to six feet (1.8m), with a spread of ten feet (3m) or more. It is the hardier of the two, and in the wild it is found as far south as Patagonia. With protection it will stand winter temperatures as cold as zero degrees Fahrenheit. The Brazilian species, which may reach eight feet (2.4m) in height, has survived winter temperatures as low as ten degrees. The frosted leaves may be folded over the crowns for protection, and extra mulch added as well. A constant supply of moisture is vital. The leaves help in this regard, functioning as giant inverse umbrellas to funnel rainwater to the interior of the plant. They need rich organic soil and spring top-dressings of rotted manure to achieve the best display. Edward Bowles stated, "I believe the great secret for insuring its reaching gigantic proportions is to 'feed the brute.' " It should go without saying that the garden must have the room for growing one.

Gardeners without a stream or pond may excavate a very large hole, up to five feet (1.5m) deep, with an equal width, fill it with good loam and compost, and plant the coconut-looking crowns in early spring, keeping everything very damp. (Or they may decide to take the plunge, and build the water feature they've been contemplating for a decade.) The gunneras are propagated by seed or careful spring division. Their name honours a man who wore two hats, J. E. Gunner, a Swedish bishop and botanist.

Heracleum Umbellifere

Another plant not for the faint of heart, or small of garden, is *Heracleum mantegazzianum*, fortunately called by its pronounceable common name of Giant Cow Parsnip. It grows by leaps and bounds to a commonly recorded height of ten feet (3m), although I've seen specimens close to twenty (6m). That the Greeks consecrated the immense plant to Hercules is no small wonder.

Giant Cow Parsnip grows wild in southeastern Europe, and it is from the Caucasus that it was introduced late in the nineteenth century. It has escaped from gardens throughout Europe. It is the tallest member of the Umbelliferae (it would quite likely be the tallest of almost any flower family) and is related to such common herbs and vegetables as dill, caraway, parsley, and celery.

The basal leaves are dark green and three feet (90cm) across, deeply divided like those of a maple. From them rise stout hollow stems, often blotched with purple, with smaller leaves. These are topped in June and July with huge round flower heads, a foot (30cm) or more across, of many tiny white blossoms. This has led to the nickname "Cartwheel Flower." It is estimated that there are ten thousand florets in just one inflorescence. For this reason, it is wise to remove the heads before they drop too many seeds. At any rate, they are excellent for large dried arrangements. (Graham Stuart Thomas recommends this plant, too, for decorating the Albert Hall.)

There is also a native British and American species, *H. sphondylium*, which was gathered for pig fodder and known as Hogweed. Those who are less than amused by self-sown seedlings of these giants growing in inappropriate spots heartily agree with the name. This variable species is found growing in many areas throughout the Northern Hemisphere, including Georgia, Alaska, Siberia, and Europe. A comparatively small plant, *H. sphondylium* grows to only eight feet (2.4m). It is found growing wild near stream beds and moist places. This Cow Parsnip is remarkably

Heracleum mantegazzianum
GIANT COW PARSNIP
Heracleum sphondylium
COW PARSNIP

LEFT, umbels of the flowers of the Giant Cow Parsnip, *H. mantegazzianum*, are held above the divided leaves, as well as the white blossoms of Mock Orange, philadelphus, and Blue Alkanet, *Anchusa azurea*. BELOW, in rich soil with ample moisture, the stout hollow stems of *H. mantegazzianum* can grow to nearly twenty feet.

similar to its Caucasian cousin, although the leaves are not as deeply carved.

Heracleums have been employed in folk healing, earning the names Masterwort, Youthwort, and Madnep. Both the roots and seeds have been used to treat colds, cramps, colic, and apoplexy. It has been further used for female complaints, and as a stimulant. The long hollow stems make exemplary peashooters. The sap of the Giant Cow Parsnip causes an allergic reaction in some people, forming blisters, so care must be taken when handling the plant and choosing its placement in the garden. Children should not play with this one.

Although they prefer moist rich soil near the waterside, Cow Parsnips will grow well enough in any sunny or partially shaded area with sufficient dampness, as is demonstrated by seedlings that sprout in moist spots. The plants are not long-lived as a rule, so it is best to grow on a few seedlings or take root cuttings. Left to its own devices, an isolated specimen in a secluded spot in the garden may turn into a bustling colony. The valuable foliage and impressive flower umbels recommend it for the back of a deep perennial border.

I received my Cow Parsnip as an unlabelled gift late one autumn. In the flurry of bulb and perennial planting, I forgot what it was, and the little tangle of white roots was stuffed desperately in a convenient bare spot and promptly forgotten. I hardly noticed a few ten-inch (25cm) leaves the next year. The third year in its very prominent spot at the front of a border, it leapt to nearly eight feet (2.4m), towering over coralbells and iris. The effect was unorthodox but dramatic.

The first *Hostas* arrived in England, brought by plant hunters from the Orient, in about 1780. At first they were thought to be exotic species of daylilies. When the differences became more apparent, they were classified as a new genus in the family Liliaceae, and named *Funkia* for the German cryptogamist Henry Funk. The name changed early in this century, and now honours Nicholaus Host, physician to the emperor of Austria at the beginning of the nineteenth century. Researchers discovered that the genus had been named for him a scant few years before it was named for Funk.

The small trumpet flowers and pleasant foliage of the first species were admired, but in a period of vast botanical exploration of the globe, unsurpassed before or since, the hostas were largely ignored. This all changed in 1830, when Dr. Philipp Franz von Siebold returned to Europe with a new species after having been expelled from Japan. (As an eye surgeon who could

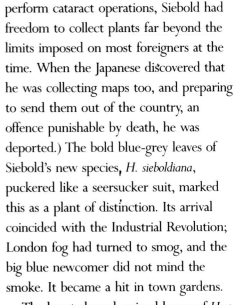

perform cataract operations, Siebold had freedom to collect plants far beyond the limits imposed on most foreigners at the time. When the Japanese discovered that he was collecting maps too, and preparing to send them out of the country, an offence punishable by death, he was deported.) The bold blue-grey leaves of Siebold's new species, *H. sieboldiana*, puckered like a seersucker suit, marked this as a plant of distinction. Its arrival coincided with the Industrial Revolution; London fog had turned to smog, and the big blue newcomer did not mind the smoke. It became a hit in town gardens.

The heart-shaped, veined leaves of *Hosta sieboldiana* are the largest and, arguably, the finest of the genus. They are broad, a foot (30cm) wide and as long, rising on long stalks from a central crown. Above the striking clumps appear dense racemes of white flowers tinged with lavender. The funnel-shaped blossoms possess a faint, sweet scent. The form most often grown, for good reason, is the selected variety 'Elegans.' Its deeply crinkled foliage appears even more blue. The leaves turn yellow in the autumn, and later the seed stalks are decorative as they poke through the snow.

When the Victorians threw themselves headlong into the fad for newfangled carpet bedding, *H. sieboldiana* and other large plants could not be regimented in such a manner, and they were relegated to the woodland, or scooped up by cottage gardeners who eschewed fashion trends. Only a generation after its introduction, the blue *Hosta* was considered an old-fashioned plant. It might have disappeared entirely but for the cottagers, and the revolutionary William Robinson and the

indomitable Miss Jekyll. Her remarkable imagination found new uses for the marvellous blue leaves, such as combining them with pale pink tree peonies. She kept a reserve supply in pots, plunking them into the inevitable bare spots that happen even to the best gardeners.

Recent years have seen a revival of interest in hostas. There are many species, and both professionals and amateurs have created worthy hybrids. Hostas are a boon to moist shady gardens. Though they will thrive in more sun if watered well, the leaves may scald in hot summers. They do best in good loamy ground and benefit from feeding. Clumps improve with time and should remain undisturbed. Hostas are very hardy, yet also thrive in southern gardens. They should not be planted in

frost pockets or warm spots where they might emerge too early and be nipped by frost, since only one set of leaves is produced, at the beginning of the season.

They have few serious pests, but slugs can spoil the leaves with unsightly holes. They are increased by division or seeds. I collected the seeds of *H. sieboldiana* from an impressive grouping in a friend's garden, where they have stood for forty years. It rarely sows itself, but these seeds germinated readily and transplanted easily. Seedlings need three years or more to attain an impressive stature.

Hosta sieboldiana
Liliaceae

PLANTAIN LILY

In a shaded grotto, OPPOSITE, the blue-green leaves of *H. sieboldiana* dominate patches of pink London Pride, *Saxifraga umbrosa*, yellow Monkey Musk, *Mimulus guttatus*, and the leaves of *Astilbe* × *arendsii*. ABOVE, *H. sieboldiana* and *Mimulus guttatus* thrive in shade. RIGHT, the lacy fronds of ferns accentuate the bold puckered leaves of *H. sieboldiana*.

The Greek name for *Hypericum* is a telling one. In some versions, *Hypereikon*, from *hyper*, above, and *eikon*, an image, denotes how the flowers have long been placed over pictures to ward off evil. Alternately, it may have been named for the Titan Hyperion, father of the Greek sun-god Helios.

It is easy to understand how this plant came to be associated with the sun. The five-petalled yellow flowers have long stamens radiating from the centre. At the end of each filamentous stamen is a bright red or golden anther of pollen. Caught by the light, they glow like a starburst, closely resembling the fibre optics of present-day technology. We might well dedicate *Hypericum* to the god of phone lines.

Early sun-worshippers in the eastern Mediterranean knew it as the sacred herb of the sun-god. It was valuable in casting spells, and was particularly revered on the summer solstice, when the sun appeared to stand still. On this Midsummer Day, bonfires were lit at sundown, worshippers sang and danced, and flower garlands of *Hypericum* were cast into the flames. The enchanted incense wafted over the frenzied revellers, symbolizing its power to exorcise evil. Gleeful Romans indulged themselves during the Feast of Fires with pagan gusto.

To the early Christian church, fun was fun, but these nature-worshipping rituals were troubling. The church "discovered" that John the Baptist just so happened to

ST. JOHN'S WORT

The entrance to a country garden, BELOW, blooms with self-sown Fumitory, *Corydalis lutea*, and St. John's Wort, *Hypericum calycinum*. OPPOSITE, St. John's Wort—with Herb Robert, *Geranium robertianum*, threading through the leaves—was by ancient peoples associated with the sun god, but later the Christian church re-christened the plant.

be born on Midsummer Day, and the Feast of Fires was converted to the Feast of St. John. *Hypericum* was re-christened St. John's Wort. "Wort" meant a healing herb, so it was declared that John had blessed the plant, enabling it to heal. Monks set to work discovering its medicinal properties; indeed, an oil extracted from the leaves and flowers was effective in relieving inflammatory problems.

But superstitions die hard. In clandestine rites throughout medieval England, bonfires glowed on the eve of the summer solstice, and debauched celebrants threw Foxglove, Monkshood, and St. John's Wort into the flames. Villagers abandoned Christian piety, at least until dawn, when morality returned. Even so, illegitimate children conceived during that night bore no stigma, as they were said to have been fathered by the sun-god.

Eventually the secret customs faded, although in America, the Pennsylvania Dutch trusted the "sacred herb" to protect newborns, and hung the flowers over their doors to keep away the evil eye.

Many species of St. John's Wort grow throughout the temperate Northern Hemisphere. *H. calycinum* originated in Asia Minor, but has long been cultivated throughout Europe, and early settlers brought it with them to America. Its large flowers, up to three inches (7.5cm) across, bloom in midsummer, as might be expected. The shrubby plants grow to only a foot and a half (45cm), and the plain olive-green leaves are evergreen in mild climates. In England it is called Rose of Sharon, although this should not be confused with the old-fashioned *Hibiscus syriacus*, which holds that name in America. *H. calycinum* is valuable for plantings in shady spots. It will also grow in more sun, and is a vigorous weed-suppressing groundcover. St. John's Wort is easily grown in average soil with ample moisture. It can be propagated from seeds or cuttings, and may be hung over the door, just in case. . . .

Hypericum calycinum Hypericaceae

There is no consensus on the origin of the name *Inula helenium* for this very old plant. Some claim it's from the Greek *inaein*, meaning "to purge," and its qualities in that area were well known. A livelier tale suggests the name may simply mean Helen's Helen—*Inula* being thought to be a corruption of *Helenula*, "little Helen"; when Paris kidnapped Helen from Troy, legend holds she had her hands full (of the bright yellow flowers). The common name is Elecampane, itself a corruption of the old, less redundant medieval Latin name *Inula campana*.

The Romans probably brought Elecampane to the British Isles, for it is found growing wild there but it is not a native. Julia, the daughter of Augustus Caesar, was said to have eaten the candied root daily to aid digestion and improve her appetite. (Julia was married three times, finally to an emperor who eventually banished her because of her licentious appetite, to an island off the west coast of Italy where she died, ironically, of starvation.) Elecampane was eaten throughout the Roman Empire as a vegetable, Turner tells how the roots were pickled, and Culpeper considered them "very effectual to warm a cold windy stomach, or the pricking therein, and stitches in the sides caused by the spleen." It was an ingredient in cough syrups until the nineteenth century.

The *Leech Book of Bald*, from 950, described in a strange melding of pagan and Christian rituals, how to use Elecampane to cure "elf disease"—madness brought on by the tricks and magic of

fairies. Timing was everything. Beginning on a Thursday evening, the formula called for impaling Elecampane with a knife, digging it up and bringing it at dawn to lay beneath the church altar, combining it with Betony and lichen taken from a crucifix, and boiling it three times with milk and holy water. The whole operation was accompanied by specific prayers and songs, and the participant was not allowed to speak to anyone. The adherence to the ritual was believed to be as important as the medicine itself.

Inula was found to be good for treating colicky horses as early as the tenth century, but with far less fuss. Hors-Helene or Horse-heal was brought to the New World for this very purpose, where it adapted well and headed for the hills. It is plentiful in the wild from Nova Scotia to North Carolina, and east to Missouri.

The leaves of Elecampane form large rosettes, and are downy on the undersides. The basal leaves grow as long as twenty inches (51cm) by eight inches (20cm) in width. Sturdy stems support branching heads of yellow flowers. The centre disc is golden, surrounded by paler short ray-florets. The flowers bloom from mid- to late summer on four- to six-foot (1.2–1.8m) stems. Elecampane is a digni-fied feature in herb gardens, or in any spot where the striking foliage and flowers can be seen to advantage. It is a gorgeous plant to position in front of yellow-green shrubs, like the cut-leaf elder or a golden juniper. The purple flowers of the butterfly bush *Buddleia davidii* bloom at the same time and are enhanced by the *Inula*'s tones. Flower arrangers enjoy the blossoms, which hold for several days in water.

The plants are easily accommodated in the garden. They are not finicky about soil, and are at home in sun or part-shade with adequate moisture. New plants can be grown from seed or root divisions, and should be given several feet of space to develop to maturity.

Inula helenium
Compositae

ELECAMPANE

BELOW, A nostalgic bouquet features *Inula helenium*, violas, Silver Lace, and lettuce flowers. LEFT, inula blooms in July.

At the beginning of the sixth century, the army of the Goths had Clovis, King of the Franks, and his men trapped at a bend in the Rhine River near Cologne. Clovis spotted the Yellow Flag, *Iris pseudacorus*, blooming far out in the river. He reasoned that the water must be shallow enough to ford, and his forces made their escape and lived to fight another day. A grateful Clovis adopted the iris as his symbol, and replaced the three toads on his coat of arms with three iris. During the Crusades, Louis VII revived it as his emblem, and it was known as Fleur de Louis, and so perhaps became Fleur de lis. The stylized design was incorporated into the royal coat of arms of England in 1340, where it remained until it was displaced by the Irish harp in 1800.

Today the heraldic symbol of kings is the same Yellow Flag found growing in English streams and rivers some thirteen hundred years after Clovis's narrow escape. The binomial designation *pseudacorus* is owing to the resemblance of the leaves to those of the Sweet Flag, *Acorus calamus*, which was a popular strewing herb. Although found growing in and near water, Fleur de lis has been grown in gardens for centuries. Gerard spoke of it in his *Herball* of 1597, saying, "Although it be a watery plant of nature, yet being planted in gardens it prospereth well."

The clumps of Yellow Flag are bold in a border if it is not too dry, on marshy banks, or in very shallow water. It is luxuriant in leaf, the tall green spears growing to four feet (1.2m). Four to twelve

Iris Iridaceae

Iris pseudacorus
FLEUR DE LIS

Iris versicolor
BLUE FLAG

Still waters suit the Fleur de lis of heraldry, Iris pseudacorus—its flowers obscured by rushlike leaves—and Water Parsnip, Sium latifolium, LEFT. The wild Blue Flag of America, Iris versicolor, BELOW, reminded settlers of its Old World counterpart.

flowers are produced on strong branching stems held among the leaves. The short upper trio of petals, called standards, are finely fringed at the top and recurve gently back into the centre of the flower. The three splayed petals, called falls, are a clear lemon colour, usually with a rippled tracery of dusky veins. The base of the petals is sometimes marked with a patch of orange, and is beardless. The flowers measure three inches (7.5cm) across and bloom in May and June. Writer Charles Grey chided his countrymen for ignoring their fair native iris, challenging, "If it came from Thibet it would certainly decorate every garden pond or stream."

The leaves were used long ago as thatch and for weaving chair seats. The seeds have been boiled as a coffee substitute, and Scots steeped the roots in water to make ink.

Thomas Jefferson recorded on May 28, 1767, that "Flower-de-luces" were "just opening" in his Monticello garden. Joseph Breck grew the "Yellow-water Iris of England" in Boston and admired the "handsome yellow flowers, the last of June. . . ." The wild iris of America, *Iris versicolor*, was called Blue Flag by nostalgic settlers after its Yellow Flag cousin. The English countryside began to feel the effects of industrialization late in the last century. Swamps and creeks were drained, and the Yellow Flag began to die out in some areas. Alarmed conservationists imported the tougher American Blue Flags, and in 1890 started a small experimental planting in the Lake District near Ullswater. Their efforts were, in fact, too successful. The Blue Flag spread far and wide. Each summer the wild flags of the two countries fly simultaneously.

Southern Africa was a gold mine to the plant hunters with its exotic flora, but the flowers were considered too tender for growing outside the greenhouse. Only much later were many plants of this region found to have a much greater tolerance to cold than had been imagined. One such case in point is the Torch Lily. The first species, *Kniphofia uvaria*, arrived in England in 1707 from the vicinity of the Cape of Good Hope. Never considering that it could be hardy, collectors coddled it as a curiosity under glass for nearly a hundred and fifty years. In 1848, a few specimens were planted outside at Kew Gardens, where they surprised everyone by surviving the winter.

In what may strike some gardeners as a deliberate case of perversity, the name was changed from the easy-to-pronounce *Tritoma*—from *tri*, three, and *tomas*, cut, referring to the three sharp edges at the points of the leaves—to the more difficult *Kniphofia*. As always, the prior name was recognized as the correct one, but we mustn't begrudge Professor J. H. Kniphof his due. In 1764, the German botanist published a spectacular twelve-volume herbal with twelve hundred illustrations reproduced by "nature printing." This exacting and laborious process took impressions from actual dried and flattened plants, later coloured by hand. Whether or not the professor managed all this work by himself is immaterial; this massive undertaking might cross the gardener's mind as he struggles with the spluttering mouthful of *Kniphofia uvaria*.

Kniphofia uvaria Liliaceae

RED-HOT POKER

Even after Kew had established the Torch Lily's garden hardiness, there were reservations. They became enormously popular in some areas, as in the west of Scotland, where they were called Bailie Nicol Jarvie's Poker, after an incident in *Rob Roy*. In Sir Walter Scott's 1818 novel, the elderly but quick-witted Jarvie is involved in a scuffle. Finding his never-used sword has rusted to its sheath, he grabs a firebrand from the hearth and sets his assailant's kilt afire. This may have captured the Scots' attention, but it is unlikely that Scots were prone to saying things like, "Oh, I see your Bailie Nicol Jarvie's Poker is in bloom," and they may have quickly adopted Red-hot-poker as the common name. William Robinson praised *K. uvaria* highly, calling it "one of the noblest and most brilliant of lily-worts."

Shirley Hibberd—a popular Victorian garden writer, who, by the way, was male—was not among the admirers, writing that there are "not many species, and the few there are, more than are wanted, from the Gardener's point of view." Nevertheless, the eye-catching Torch Lily fascinated impressionable Victorians, and many hybrids were produced, with *K. uvaria* figuring prominently in their parentage. Fifty varieties were available, and

Hibberd continued to see red, warning that the Torch Lilies made "a fiery glow in the shrubbery borders and a regular conflagration in the parterre."

Almost all of these hybrids are lost, but the species survived, and plantsmen have created new hybrids in this century. The smooth flower stems rise from yucca-like spikes of dark green leaves. The flame-coloured, two-inch (5cm) flowers are packed tightly at the top of the stems, rising up to five feet (1.5m) and indeed resembling burning torches. The tubular flowers at the bottom gradually shade to pale cream, as if they have not yet "caught fire." The flowers are produced in summer, sometimes well into autumn. Peter Henderson, who noted that fellow Americans called it Flame Flower, wrote that *K. uvaria* was "a plant admirably adapted for single clumps on the lawn, or among shrubbery, where its tall spikes of orange-red flowers make an effective display from August to December." The flower stems can be cut for dramatic and long-lasting decorations.

The leaves are more or less evergreen, according to climate, but spread out in winter, allowing water to gather in the crown. The plants may suffer great damage if the water freezes, so it is best to protect the crowns with a mulch. Some tie the leaves together at the top to shed rain away from the centre. The Torch Lily benefits from a position on a bank where excess moisture does not collect, or in a moderately dry bed with free-draining soil of average fertility. Full sun is preferable, and the plants should remain undisturbed. To propagate, divide the clumps in spring or sow seeds, which take at least three years to reach flowering size.

It was originally doubted that the Red-hot poker, *Kniphofia uvaria*, OPPOSITE, which was discovered in southern Africa, would prove hardy in temperate climates, but evidence that it is indeed cold-tolerant is found in charming gardens everywhere.

Lavandula angustifolia
Labiatae

ENGLISH LAVENDER

ABOVE, Romans may have introduced *Lavandula angustifolia* to England, where it remains an intrinsic feature of gardens, such as for edging beds of roses.

Lavender is the quintessential herb of English gardens, where it has grown from time immemorial. *Flora Domestica*, a charming English book published anonymously in 1823, evokes its timeless aura in simple terms: "Pure Lavender, to lay in bridal gown." From the grandest manor to the humblest cottage, Lavender has always been in fashion since it was introduced at a point lost in early history. *Lavandula angustifolia* is the English Lavender, which came from the sunny Mediterranean, although some botanists suspect it may have originated long ago in India. The name comes from the Latin *lavandus*, meaning "to be washed," for Roman bathers used the oil to perfume their baths. The Romans may well have brought Lavender to Britain.

Lavender was so popular by William Turner's day, that in 1568 he wrote it was "but lost labor, to describe them that are so well knowen al redy." The ornamental value of Lavender was scarcely considered at first. Turner suggested sprigs of the flowers could be "quilted in a cappe and dayle worne for all the diseases of the head that come of a cold cause, and comforte the brayne very well." Lavender salts have long been used to stimulate those in danger of fainting—John Gerard said it might bring relief for "them that use to swoune much." He also claimed Lavender would still "the panting and passion of the hart," as if anyone would seek a cure for love. (One shudders at what ills Culpeper might have suggested Lavender to cure; happily, he didn't.)

When knot gardens came into vogue, Lavender was sometimes used, and it was shorn into short silver hedges. This necessitated growing plants in two separate areas, for according to John Reid in *The Scots Garden* of 1766, "but for the sake of the flowers, which are often used, we must have a plantation of it apart; for were the edging plants suffered to flower, their beauty would be spoiled." Not all thought the clipped forms the fairest. Queen Henrietta Maria is said to have especially fancied a white-flowering variety.

The flowers were gathered and pressed to obtain the uniquely scented oil. Lavender water, as it is called, consisted of the spirits of wine scented with the oil, and was a popular perfume. It was said to banish blemishes and puffiness. During the reign of Elizabeth I, perfume was used instead of soap, which needed to be imported at great expense from the Continent. James I had a virtual monopoly on soap-making in his day. When his fortunes waned, he sold his soap holdings in 1671 to William Yardley of Surrey. It was Yardley who added the essence of Lavender to his soap, starting a long tradition and contributing to a sweeter-smelling populace.

It has been a custom until the present day to place Lavender in chests to repel insects and sweeten the contents; Lavender-scented sheets were highly esteemed. Joseph Breck related that it was a common custom "to scatter the flowers over linen, as some do rose leaves, for the sake of their sweet odor." Sprinkling Lavender over the head would keep one chaste, not to mention mothproof.

Although the French have had a thriving Lavender-growing industry for hundreds of years, plants raised in England were considered to contain more oil of a richer scent, and were sold at a higher price. It may be surmised that the aromatic oil evaporates more quickly in a hot, dry region.

Lavender plants crossed the Atlantic early on, but they often needed protection to survive the harsher winters, especially in New England. Breck encountered the problem in Boston, and had come to terms with it, writing, "In cold, moist soil, it is almost sure to be winter-killed; but in a dry, loamy, or gravelly soil, it endures our winters with but little protection. We have been successful in the cultivation of it in a soil of the latter quality, and, from the flowers that grew upon the edging of a circular bed, six feet in diameter, obtained more than one ounce of the pure Lavender, one drop of which would perfume a room." Breck was incredibly industrious, and his cultural instructions are still valid.

Lavandula angustifolia (which previously was classified as *L. spica* or *L. vera*) needs abundant sunshine, and is drought-tolerant. It is virtually immune from pests. The small shrubs reach from a foot and a half to three feet. Old woody growth should be pruned away only in the early spring to promote bushiness. The shock of radical pruning is reported to kill old plants. The flowers should be picked in the morning, just as the buds open, when the fragrance is at its peak. The thin leaves (the binomial *angustifolia* refers to the narrow foliage) and bracketed blue flower spikes have an overall gray cast. Lavender is delightful planted anywhere in the garden, but is its most elegant in association with roses.

Flowers of *Lavandula angustifolia* grown in England, ABOVE, are the most valued for their rich concentration of oils. BELOW, Lavender-scented linens are a luxury within every gardener's reach; it is best to harvest the flowers in the morning when their scent is richest.

The reputation of lilies was tarnished considerably in the first half of this century, when boatloads of soft, sick bulbs of Oriental species flooded the markets of America and England. The subsequent failures branded lilies in general as difficult, and many gardeners avoided them like the plague. This was a pity, because few other flowers had fuelled the imaginations of artists and gardeners alike for so many countless generations.

Lilium candidum may be the oldest of domesticated flowers. Its country of origin is not certain, but is probably in the Balkans. It decorates Cretan pottery that is nearly three thousand years old. It is clearly described by Dioscorides. The Phoenicians may be responsible for spreading it throughout the Mediterranean basin. The Romans cultivated the White Lily, and it received the designation *candidum*, meaning "shining white," from the poet Virgil. Heresy though it may seem, it was valued because the bulbs were eaten or used medicinally. Wild populations of this lily throughout Europe suggest that the Romans planted it near permanent military camps; it was used to break boils and treasured as a cure for corns, which may have come in handy for the foot soldiers.

Its association with the Virgin Mary dates from the second century, when the tradition of her Assumption gained currency; on the third day following her burial, her tomb was found empty except for lilies and roses, her body having ascended to heaven. It became Mary's emblem in paintings, the white petals symbolizing the Virgin's purity and the golden anthers her heavenly soul (and, presumably, the fragrance her sweet grace). The White Lily—strangely, it wasn't called the Madonna Lily until the late nineteenth century—was grown in every English monastery garden, both to treat cuts and sores, and to decorate the chapel. The so-called Easter Lily of today, *L. longiflorum*, is native to Taiwan, and is a rather more coarse variation on the same theme, its large funnel-shaped flowers better seen from the back pews.

The Old White Lily, as it was called, had arrived in America by 1630. Eighteenth- and nineteenth-century gardeners grew a pink-striped variety and a double-flowered form, a classic near case of gilding the lily, which has been lost to few regrets. Breck disdained the variegated variety as "not very desirable," and of the double form said simply, "It is a monster, and for that reason may be fancied by some." The Madonna Lily survived the Victorian era sequestered in cottage gardens. There the undisturbed bulbs thrived, possibly from the housewife's custom of flinging her pails of soapy water on the plants, thereby killing virus-spreading aphids and preventing fungal infections.

The Turk's-cap Lily, *L. martagon*, may be a British wildflower, but is more likely a

Lilium Liliaceae

Lilium candidum MADONNA LILY

Lilium hansonii HANSON'S LILY

Lilium martagon TURK'S-CAP LILY

very early immigrant from Germany and France. Turner was under the erroneous impression that it had originated in the Mideast and been brought to Constantinople for the gardens of the sultans; this fostered the notion that the flowers resembled Turk's caps. The word "martagon" may be derived from the Turkish *martagan*, a turban worn by Sultan Muhammad I, who ruled the Ottoman Empire in the fifteenth century.

Although the typical colour of the spotted flowers is plum pink, a number of variations were known in Parkinson's time, including the white form called 'Album,' and a deep maroon labelled 'Cattaniae.'

L. hansonii first flowered in England in 1871. It was named for artist Peter Hanson of Brooklyn, New York, who had one of the finest collections of lilies in the world. It was called Japanese Turk's-cap, a rather odd cross-cultural muddle, further belied by the fact it was discovered in Korea. The golden flowers, flushed with citrus orange, resemble those of the European Martagon Lily. They measure two inches (5cm) across, and the recurved petals are sprinkled with purplish-brown spots. They carry a light sweet scent. Despite their present geographic isolation from each other, *L. hansonii* and *L. martagon* are closely allied. This is demonstrated by the ease with which they can be hybridized. Mr. and Mrs. R. O. Backhouse were English gardeners extraordinaire, and their beautiful crosses involving the two species were created before the turn of the century. The Backhouse Hybrids are still grown.

These two species also exhibit traits quite different from most other lilies found in the garden. The leaves are held in

ILLUSTRATION, OPPOSITE, the Madonna Lily, *Lilium candidum*, is one of the oldest cultivated flowers. OPPOSITE LEFT, the golden orange pendant flowers of *Lilium hansonii* show to advantage in partially shaded garden areas. OPPOSITE RIGHT, the white form of *Lilium martagon* 'Album' was known by Parkinson, and is lovely growing among ferns. ABOVE, the typical colour of Turk's-cap, *Lilium martagon*, is plum pink and, as a wild flower of central Europe, thrives in alkaline soils in dappled shade.

whorls, rather than arranged alternately along the stems, suggesting that in evolutionary terms, they are older. Both actually thrive in alkaline soil, as does *L. candidum*, a boon to gardeners on chalk. The entire genus requires superior drainage in loose, friable soil, but these three are the most adaptable and will accept a stiffer loam.

The Madonna Lily grows in full sun to a height of four to five feet (1.2–1.5m). The pristine flowers bloom in June. Bulbs are planted during their dormant period in August. They differ from every other lily in that they are planted with just a scant covering of soil, less than an inch (2.5cm), over their noses. After a rest, the bulbs form a rosette of leaves that persists through the winter, and should be shielded from collected moisture. They frustrate some, who may not be in the habit of

tossing their wash water into the garden.

Martagons reach three to five feet (90cm–1.5m) in height, and twenty or thirty waxy pendant flowers are borne on each stem in June and July. They do best in a facsimile of their wild habitat, where they thrive in partial shade. Bulbs are planted about six inches (15cm) deep in autumn or spring, and take several years to settle in, often remaining dormant the first season. Martagon Lilies will persist in the garden for many years without special attention. The white form 'Album' is lovely with ferns. *L. hansonii* is treated in a similar fashion. The golden-orange flowers are luminous set against dark shrubbery. Four-foot (1.2m) stems bear up to a dozen nodding blooms. I know of a clump planted a half-century ago that thrives in the lacy shade of a Honey Locust tree.

Lychnis coronaria, it was told, sprang from the bath water of Aphrodite. It is unclear whether the lady, who was born of seafoam herself, was startled, as well she might have been by the shocking magenta flowers. We do know that, on that day at least, she was bathing somewhere in Bulgaria, from whence the plant originated. Pliny thought it, despite its scentless state, to be a rose, and the flowers were woven into garlands to adorn the champions, or campions, of athletic contests. The so-named Rose Campion spread throughout Europe. It was the first of its genus to be named *Lychnis*, or Lamp Flower, because the hairs of the leaves were gathered and burnt as lamp wicks.

L. coronaria was grown in England by the mid-fourteenth century, under the name Rose-Campy, when spelling was more creative. It was locally called Gardner's-delight, Dutch Christ's Eie (eye), and Bachelor's-buttons, though this alliterative name has been bestowed indiscriminately on many flowers. Thomas Fairchild recognized Rose Campion, in his 1722 volume *The City Gardiner*, as an outstanding plant for London conditions. He cautioned people to buy freshly dug plants from reputable nurseries, for "I and others have seen Plants that were to be sold in the Markets, that were as uncertain of Growth as a piece of Noah's Ark would be, had we it here to plant." Modern gardeners who receive dried-out root stock can at least take solace in the problem being an old one.

The white-flowered sport appeared by

Lychnis Caryophyllaceae

Lychnis chalcedonica JERUSALEM CROSS

Lychnis coronaria ROSE CAMPION

1600, and double-flowered varieties of both magenta and white were the rage in the eighteenth century, but seem to be extinct. About 1750, 'The Painted Lady Rose-Campion' was sold by Mr. Drummond, a seed merchant of Edinburgh. It seems to correspond to a white variety with a cerise eye grown today. The Rose Campion transplanted well to North American shores, and sometimes still forms small colonies of its own in the wild.

Controversy has long swirled in fashionable circles over the riotous magenta colour of the original form. Its fortune rose and fell with garden trend-setters; some branded the flowers, which were widely grown and inexpensive, as vulgar. Shirley Hibberd would have no such nonsense, declaring, "Whoever would despise them for their cheapness would deserve to see no more flowers in this world, whatever he might see in the other."

The intense colours of *Lychnis coronaria* are paired with *Ballota pseudodictamnus*, OPPOSITE. Antique measures, ABOVE, hold Rose Campion, Edelweiss, *Leontopodium alpinum*, Fernbush, *Chamaebatiaria millefolium*, *Geranium cantabridgense*, and sage leaves. The double form of *L. chalcedonica*, BELOW, has been preserved by careful propagation.

L. chalcedonica is another species of great antiquity. Though a native of Russia, it was grown in gardens of the Turks, and quite likely travelled with returning Crusaders throughout Europe. This theory is supported by the fact it is called Jerusalem-cross in France, Spain, Italy, and Germany, as well as England. The brilliant vermillion flowers are shaped like a Maltese cross, by which name it is known in Portugal. Chalcedon was a city at the entrance to the Bosporus, and *chalcedonica* refers to the plant's Turkish connections, as well as its colour—*khalkos* is Greek for copper.

It was an immediate sensation in England, where its fiery colour stood alone in early summer. It received many folk names as it spread throughout the island, such as Campion of Constantinople, Scarlet Lightning, and Bridget-in-her-bravery. The latter commemorates the Irish saint who was not burned at the stake, as one might think from the flower's colour, but stood up for justice. The town of Bristol, known for its red cloth, took it as an unofficial emblem, and in the vicinity it was called Flower of Bristow (Bristol).

The double-flowered 'Rubra Plena' was known by 1629, and Parkinson was ecstatic. "This glorious flower being as rare as it is beautiful," he wrote, "so for his bravery deserves a Master of account that will take care to keepe and preserve it." It is a bit miraculous that it has survived, since while the single form comes easily from seed, the double Jerusalem-cross is multiplied only by division or cuttings. It was available in the United States by 1850, as was a double white that has not been reported since the First World War in either country. 'Rubra Plena' is still rare.

These two *Lychnis* species have survived nearly four hundred years of cultivation in foreign lands because they are tough. A half day's sun is the minimal requirement, and they need little attention. *L. coronaria* grows to two feet (60cm) in height and thrives even in poor, relatively dry soil. The basal clumps of leaves appear as if cut from grey flannel. The flowers recommend themselves with a long display of bloom during summer. Their colour cannot be denied. Rose Campions are lovely in a garden vignette with pale pink cranesbills, the white form of the ever-blooming Bleeding-heart, *Dicentra eximia*, and royal blue larkspurs.

Jerusalem-cross, *L. chalcedonica*, grows to four feet (1.2m) and forms thick, long-lived clumps. It is extremely hardy, blooming profusely in mountain gardens at 10,000 feet (3,000m).

Lysimachia **Primulaceae**

Lysimachia clethroides OLD GOOSENECK

Lysimachia punctata CIRCLE FLOWER

Legend tells how a brave king of Thrace stopped a rampaging bull cold in his tracks by waving a stem of Yellow Loosestrife in his face. Sixteenth-century translations of the writings of Pliny the Elder reveal that "it retaineth and keepeth the name of King Lysimachus . . . the first finder-out of the nature and vertues of this herb." Sprays of *Lysimachia* could be laid across the shoulders of quarrelling teams of oxen to reconcile them—they would "lose strife." The oxen would also cease to be bothered by insects, who are repelled by the scent of the plant. In his play *The Faithful Shepherdess*, John Fletcher wrote,

"Yellow lysimachus, to give sweet rest
To the faint shepherd, killing, where it comes,
All busy gnats and every fly that hums."

Stems were hung from ceiling beams in days past to keep away flies, and it could be burned for the same purpose, as well as to drive away serpents. Pliny had observed that snakes "craule away at the smell" and, on another practical note, "it dieth haire yellow, which is not very unlike to be done by reason the flowres are yellow." The image of bleached-blond Greeks is an unusual one today, although Helen of Troy had golden hair, and Greek and Roman satirists joked about "hair out of a bottle."

L. punctata was grown in English gardens at least by 1820, but may have been introduced much earlier. This native of Asia Minor closely resembles the wild British species, *L. vulgaris*, so confusion has arisen over which plant is meant in older sources. Circle Flower, as the newcomer

was called, opted for life in the wild as well, and is found growing at pondside and in ditches in Europe and parts of America. In the garden it forms three-foot (90cm)-tall clumps of bright yellow flowers in summer. Individual blossoms, an inch (2.5cm) across, are clustered in whorls close to the stem. Each circle of flowers is delineated by a base of olive-green leaves.

A white species from China came to gardens in 1869. *L. clethroides* possessed the charm and constitution of an instant classic. Its numerous five-petalled flowers, almost a half-inch (1cm) in diameter, are held in slender racemes. These racemes reminded botanists of those of the shrub

Clethra, hence the name *clethroides*. At flowering time the spikes arch gracefully —all in the same direction, as if caught in a perpetual stiff breeze. It received the fanciful names of Old Gooseneck and Shepherd's-crook. Peter Henderson recommended it to American gardeners more than a hundred years ago, describing it as "a graceful and beautiful plant, from two to three feet high, bearing long dense nodding spikes of white blossoms, the leaves displaying brilliant tints in autumn."

The needs of Circle Flower are simple, as it adapts to sun or part-shade in most soils. The stems of yellow flowers are of good value in filtered light, where they

Its running rootstock enables Circle Flower, *Lysimachia punctata*, to cover large areas of moist ground in woodland gardens, OPPOSITE. ILLUSTRATION, TOP, *Lysimachia clethroides* is fancifully called Old Gooseneck. BELOW, a confetti of petals from an overhanging rose falls upon *Lysimachia punctata* flowering on a pondside bank.

look at home behind the foliage of hostas, or with Feverfew. The plants are divided easily in spring or autumn, or may be rooted from cuttings or grown from seed.

Old Gooseneck is unique and invaluable in the late summer border for its profusion of white arching heads. Large drifts add a sensation of motion to a planting, suggesting white-capped waves. The slightly greyed cast of the flowers is effective with pink, such as the coneflower *Echinacea purpurea*, and the pink form of Baby's Breath. It is equally striking with the steely blues of sea hollies and the globe thistle *Echinops ritro*. The flowers are whimsical additions to bouquets.

Both the lysimachias have been criticized for the invasiveness of their running rootstocks. This is somewhat unfair, for in drier conditions they are models of decorum. They are rampant only in moist soils, where they may form sizable colonies. Yellow swathes of Circle Flower are often pleasant features in partially shaded woodland gardens. They are admirable for controlling erosion on banks. It is up to the gardener to position *Lysimachia* where it is best suited given his particular rainfall and soil type. I am reminded of a friend who gardens on poor soil, in shade, and owns a wolfhound (she claims *borzoi* is Russian for backhoe). She seeks out flowers that succeed in these circumstances, and Circle Flower and Old Gooseneck prosper despite her challenges.

LEFT, a baritone tuba blasts an armful of *Lysimachia clethroides* flowers into the air. The gracefully arching spikes of **Old Gooseneck**, *Lysimachia clethroides*, OPPOSITE, provide a sense of perpetual motion in the garden.

Malva alcea is the pink Mallow grown in English perennial gardens for nearly two hundred years. The plant grows wild in many parts of Europe, including France, Belgium, and Denmark. The five-petalled pink flowers are decidedly old-fashioned, and look at home in picket-fenced gardens surrounding white clapboard houses. Beyond their beauty is a family with an interesting history.

The mallows are an enormous family of plants that includes *Malva*, *Althaea*, and *Lavatera*. Among them are *Althaea rosea*, the Hollyhock, long a darling of gardeners, and *Althaea officinalis*, the Marsh Mallow. Its roots supplied the mucilaginous juice used to make the sweet confections, although gum arabic provided a cheaper substitute, and gelatin cheaper still. The leaves and roots of mallows were eaten and employed in many medicinal ways. The Italian botanist Petri Andreae Matthioli, physician to Emperor Maximilian II, wrote in the mid-sixteenth century of their value, instructing, "The raw leaves mashed with a little salt and honey cure the fistulas in the eyes which come close to the nose. Applied to the stings of the wasp or honey-flies, they are very good." He also told how the leaves could be cooked, mixed with oil, and applied to the outbreaks of St. Anthony's Fire, or erysipelas, an infectious skin disease.

The emollient properties found in mallows were effective against insect bites, burns, and sore throats. Taken internally, mallow decoctions were used in cases of kidney stones, constipation, and gonorrhea. The stalks and leaves were boiled and drunk by pregnant women to speed delivery, and by nursing mothers to increase their milk. And, supposed miracle of miracles, mallow salve was said to prevent baldness.

In the wild, the pink Mallow is variable. The erect form of *Malva alcea*, called 'Fastigiata,' was first grown in 1820 and is most often seen. It was grown in North America by 1850; Joseph Breck said it originated in Germany. The upright branching stems, growing to three feet (90cm), are clad with lobed leaves. The pink cup-shaped flowers are produced in clusters throughout the upper branches. Resembling small hollyhocks, the satiny blooms have five slightly ruffled petals, and a protruding centre dusted with ivory-coloured pollen. The bloom season is a long one, from June to August or later.

In the garden, pink Mallow is pretty combined with deeper pink flowers, such as phlox, and pale-toned daylilies or yarrow. The flowers are dramatic against dark shrubs. The plants are sun-loving, and they perform best in average soil supplemented with compost or manure. The pink Mallow is winter-hardy and is not prone to problems. Propagation is by spring or autumn division, or by seed. They rarely seed themselves, although the most vigorous specimen I've ever grown volunteered in a bed of squash.

Malva alcea
Malvaceae

MALLOW

OPPOSITE, a classic colour scheme incorporates *M. alcea* 'Fastigiata', *Achillea* × *taygetea* 'Sheilagh', and *Phlox paniculata*. RIGHT, blossoms of *M. alcea* 'Fastigiata' are backed by *Cotinus coggygria*. LEFT, *A. officinalis* was the source for the confections.

For centuries gardeners have known that when transplanted, Catnip is at the mercy of cats, while direct-sown seedlings are usually not touched by them.

Since at least 1265, gardeners have found peculiar pleasure observing the uninhibited behaviour of their pets in a Catnip stupor. *Nepeta cataria*, the Wild Catnip of the British Isles, is an unassuming plant with sprays of small white flowers and a powerful attraction—to cats, anyway. In 1700, in *The Compleat Herbal*, the botanist J. Pitton de Tournefort described how French felines reacted to *Nepeta*, saying, "when a Cat has smelt it (even before she has well seen it) hugg'd it and kiss'd it, wantonly running upon it and scouring away from it by turns, and has rub'd herself against it very much and long, using strange Postures and playing with it, she at last eats it up and devours it entirely." That pretty much sums it up—we love to watch normally aloof cats make fools of themselves.

Catnip or Catmint—take your pick—was also believed to have an effect on humans. The meek were said to be emboldened by eating the plant. Tournefort told the tale of an executioner "that was otherwise gentle and pusillanimous, who never had the Courage to behead or hang any One, till he had first chewed the Root of Catmint." The juice of Catmint combined with oil of rose was an old treatment to remove scars. Tea made from the leaves and flowers is tangy and refreshing, and no human urges to claw furniture are reported.

Graceful sprays of Catmint, *Nepeta × faasenii*, are combined in a brightly gazed pot with Foxglove, *Digitalis purpurea*, and Jewel Weed, *Impatiens capensis*, ABOVE. Plumes of Catmint bloom with *Dianthus arenarius* 'White Lace' in June, BELOW.

Catmints are members of the mint family, Labiatae. The name *Nepeta* is of uncertain origin, although it may be derived from the ancient Etruscan city of Nepete, possibly overrun with cats.

The mauve Catmint of gardens is *Nepeta × faassenii*, a very old, and accidental, hybrid between the European species *N. mussinii* and *N. nepetella*. It has been known since 1784, and the ethereal sprays of flowers have been indispensable ever since. The small serrated grey leaves of the bushy plants are topped in June by a display so profuse as to appear as clouds of lavender-blue mist. Gertrude Jekyll's practice was to ensure a long season of bloom from Catmint. She wrote, "Its normal flowering time is June, but it is cut half back, removing the first bloom, by the middle of the month, when it at once makes new flowering shoots." Thus treated, it may continue to flower well into the fall. There is no reason to leave the spent flowers anyway, since *N. × faassenii* is sterile. The erect stems grow up to twenty inches (50cm), with an equal spread. Several forms and hybrids of garden origin, such as the 'Six Hills Giant,' are often grown.

The true *N. mussinii*, for which the hybrid is often mistaken, has a loose, more prostrate habit and grows a foot (30cm) high. Its lavender flowers set seed freely. Siberian Catmint, *N. siberica*, arrived in England in 1760. The flowers are freely borne on three-foot (90cm) stems, and provide a cool note in midsummer.

The lavender Catmint is not as powerful an attraction as the wild sort, but cats love to roll in it, and being sterile, it can't be

Nepeta Labiatae

Nepeta cataria
WILD CATNIP

Nepeta x faassenii
CATMINT

Nepeta siberica
SIBERIAN CATMINT

There's an old saying about growing Catnip:

If you set it, the cats will get it;
If you sow it, the cats won't know it.

ABOVE, lavender *Nepeta siberica* skirts clumps of Oriental Poppies, Goatsbeard, and Cranesbill.

seeded. A few strategically placed rose canes may do the trick, or a separate area may be set aside where the wild species is grown for the cat's pleasure alone. The flowers of both plants are favourites of bees, leading to some interesting confrontations. My neighbour grows *N. cataria* in hanging baskets to provide a continuous supply for his cats throughout the summer. Even these have been known to mysteriously crash to the ground; nobody has figured out how the clever and adroit cats have managed to dislodge the pots from their eight-foot (2.4m)-high perch. The aromatic flowers of Catmints may be added to arrangements, but only in houses secured against neighbourhood tabbies, as I have learned the hard way.

Regardless of whether the gardener has or desires cats, *Nepeta* is effective in the perennial border or the herb garden. In late Victorian times Catmint was occasionally bedded out in rows and geometric designs. The pale lavender colour is valuable in pastel colour schemes, such as with Lamb's-ears, *Stachys byzantina*, and pink roses and cranesbills. The flowers of Catmint are also pretty combined with those of deeper purple, like sages or iris, or with blossoms of crimson or orange.

Hardy even in very cold winters, *N. × faassenii* and *N. mussinii* are nonetheless intolerant of poorly drained situations and may die in winter. The key, once again, is quick-draining soil on the dry side. Full sun is advisable. Planting, division, and cutting back dead stems are chores best left for spring. Wild Catmint flourishes with less sunshine and more water.

The genus *Origanum* is favoured for culinary purposes, but the marjorams, or oreganos, are ornamental plants in their own right. The name is derived from *origanon*, the Greek word for these aromatic members of the mint family, and was said to mean "joy of the mountains." More than thirty joyful species are found throughout Europe and Asia, but they are especially prominent, as one might expect, in the Mediterranean region.

The Greeks put great store in the herb, and it was believed that *Origanum* derived its scent from being touched by Venus. Newlyweds were crowned with wreaths of the stems. In the belief that the dead would not sleep in peace without it, *Origanum* was planted on graves.

The names "Oregano" and "Marjoram" are used somewhat interchangeably, although the latter is usually associated today with *O. majorana*, Sweet Marjoram, a tender perennial grown as an annual. The sort dried and sold for flavouring pasta and pizza is *O. vulgare*, which grows wild in Europe, including England, and is now naturalized in parts of America. To confuse matters, it is often called Wild Marjoram. It is characterized by the tiny pink flowers on wiry stems, which long ago yielded a mauve dye. A tea brewed from the dried leaves was said to be "exceedingly grateful," although I was not, when I mistook them for those of Peppermint and made myself a cup—tastes seem to have changed over the last three hundred years.

Culpeper concluded that Wild Marjoram was an antidote for snakebite—but

Origanum Labiatae

Origanum dictamnus
DITTANY OF CRETE

Origanum vulgare
OREGANO

ILLUSTRATION, TOP, *Origanum vulgare*.
Dittany of Crete, *Origanum dictamnus*, is grown in pots in cold-winter gardens, OPPOSITE.

then there were few plants he did not recommend for this purpose. In a more useful vein, it was later reputed to have a sedative effect on sexual urges; the discoverer of this attribute was a clergyman who ran an asylum for orphans.

O. dictamnus made its way from the Isle of Crete to England very early. An early cookbook, from the fifteenth century, calls for Dytayn in recipes. Other names included "Organy" and "Dittany of Crete," by which we know it today. Apart from its flavour, it had the unusual virtue that if a goat wounded by an arrow ate Dittany, the arrow would fall out. This had broader applications than one might assume, and William Turner in 1551 instructed how to use it to extract splinters and thorns. He also related that ". . . if the smel of it come unto venemous beastes, it driveth them awaye, and if it be hanged about them, it killeth them. . . ." Tournefort discounted this in his herbal of 1700, saying, "This is too much to be true. . . ."

Even so, sprigs of Dittany of Crete were hung in rooms up until early Victorian days to keep away flies and other "venemous beastes."

Wild Marjoram, while not in the forefront of showy flowers, is rarely out of bloom all summer. The pink flowers, about a quarter of an inch (6mm) across, are borne in loose racemes on erect stems up to two feet (60cm) tall. The stems and flower bracts are dark-tinted, giving an overall dusty purple tone. They associate comfortably with the silver foliage of Snow-in-summer, *Cerastium tomentosum*, and many varieties of pinks. A notable variety is 'Aureum' with distinct chartreuse-yellow leaves. Its colour, which is more brilliant when the plant is grown in full sun, may work to accent the brilliant hues of thrift *Armeria maritima* or of Coralbells. In addition, the leaves may enliven the sombre-toned foliage of purple-leaved sages or bronze Fennel. Wild Marjoram is very hardy, and requires a mostly sunny spot in average or even poor soils. Volunteer seedlings are likely to seed themselves in a picturesque manner. Although bees work the flowers industriously, I wonder about the taste of the resulting honey.

The woolly white leaves of Dittany of Crete are beautifully mottled. They are arranged on the stiff stems somewhat like eucalyptus leaves. The tiny pink flowers dangle from overlapping bracts that change to deep rose as they mature. Dittany of Crete has a strong constitution but even so, it is not winter-hardy in climates colder than Washington, D.C. For this reason it is often grown in terra-cotta pots that can be moved inside. It is rarely used for cooking, though it is an ingredient in vermouth.

Phygelius capensis
Scrophulariaceae

The exploration of the southern part of Africa uncovered a diverse flora of exotic beauty. Treasure after treasure arrived on British shores, not the least among them *Phygelius capensis* in 1850, christened the Cape Figwort. In South Africa it carries the pretty name "River Bells," as it can be found growing wild on the banks of streams and rivers. The botanical name is of Greek origin, but the meaning is somewhat obscure. A best guess is that it means "shade-lover," from *phyge*, flight, and *helios*, the sun. Since the plant loves a sunny position, it might also be construed that the tall plants fly to, rather than from, the sun. *Capensis* refers to the area of the Cape of Good Hope as its home.

It is a member of the family Scrophulariaceae, which includes such garden favourites as foxgloves, penstemons, veronica, and snapdragons. River Bells tower above them all, sometimes achieving eight feet in favourable locations. It is understandable that it should attract admiration and become popular. The paintings of Alice Drummond-Hay, an amateur artist who, about 1890, chronicled the flowers growing in the gardens of her family home in Perthshire, Scotland, have recently come to light. In one, *Phygelius* is clearly depicted in a watercolour with Baby's Breath and *Digitalis grandiflora*. It demonstrates that River Bells were widely grown in the British Isles even in areas of winter cold. *Phygelius* was growing in America at least by the time Alice Drummond-Hay painted it in her Scottish garden.

In mild climates, *Phygelius* produces

RIVER BELLS

The tubular bells of *Phygelius capensis* curve inward toward the stem, OPPOSITE, and are arranged with seed heads of *Thalictrum aquilegifolium*, lavender *Agastache foeniculum*, and the spotted leaves of *Pulmonaria officinalis*. BELOW, River Bells, *Phygelius capensis*, form tall clumps up to six feet tall.

woody stems that remain from year to year. In colder localities, it is cut to the ground each winter, sending up slender leafy stems annually. The glossy dark leaves resemble those of fuchsias. The many-tiered inflorescence is like a candelabrum. The drooping tubular flowers of coral red swing back towards the stem. The colour is more intense in the interior of the trumpets; the pointed petals open to display the yellow throat. The variety 'Coccineus' is brilliant scarlet with a deeper yellow throat, but otherwise similar. Flowers are produced from midsummer until frost. River Bells are decorative additions to plantings with late-blooming lilies and asters. They are often situated against south-facing walls, where the intriguing flower stems make a strong architectural statement. Clumps expand slowly to three or four feet across.

Hardiness can't be guaranteed in all gardens, but *Phygelius* survives tough Colorado winters planted in gritty, well-drained soil. Failures may result from planting in wet clay. The plants should be well watered in periods of drought and high temperatures. Sun is preferable, but the plants tolerate partial shade. Stem cuttings may be rooted to produce more plants, though it is the large garden indeed that can accommodate many River Bells.

Platycodon grandiflorus
Campanulaceae

BALLOON FLOWER

But for a quirk of its seed capsules, this flower would be one among the hundreds of plants in the genus *Campanula*. Instead, botanists assigned it to its own genus, *Platycodon*, of which there is only one species, *grandiflorus*. Enthusiasts might well argue that the distinction is a deserving one, but perhaps not from the hair-splitting botanic reason (the capsules open from valves at the top, as opposed to pores in the side in *Campanula*). This is one of the few flowers, among which rose might be included, where the buds are as highly praised as the flowers. In the case of *Platycodon*, the swelling buds puff up like a hot-air balloon. Few common names are as singularly appropriate as Balloon Flower. The Latin name comes from *platys*, meaning broad, and *kodon*, a bell, which describes the flowers well enough, but once again completely misses the point.

Balloon Flower originated in China and Siberia, and officially was introduced to English horticulture in 1782, although it is possible that Gerard's "Blew Bell-flower of China" may have been *Platycodon*. This would set the date back to 1597, although the plant would surely have been very rare. An expedition of Russian naturalists to Siberia found the plant growing wild, and Johann Gmelin published his account of their findings in 1754. We may count ourselves lucky that the genus was not named for him. *Platycodon* was lost to cultivation, but was re-introduced by Robert Fortune after his 1842 trip to China.

The original species has a sprawling habit. When the famous nurseryman Sir

J. H. Veitch sent the collector Charles Maries to Japan, he returned in 1879 with a compact version. The variety 'Mariesii' superseded the original, and is a classic today. 'Mariesii' was quickly shipped to New England, and Peter Henderson wrote in 1890 of "a new dwarf variety from Japan . . . a distinct and most acceptable border plant." Balloon Flowers were said to cover some Japanese valleys as the heather carpets the Scottish moors. They figured in Oriental medicine, and were substituted, by design or accident, for the roots of ginseng in shipments to the West.

The plants emerge comparatively late in the spring. The leaves on the two-foot (60cm) stems are blue-green. The flowers bloom over many weeks in late summer. The tiny buds are pale green at first, but as they inflate change to lavender. The petals display darker purple veins inside and out. Children are likely to pop all of the fattest buds, which is hard on the flowers. When allowed to open of their own accord (few gardeners of any age can resist popping just one or two), the flowers measure from two to three inches (5–7.5cm) across and are slightly down-facing. This old-time favourite is a natural for the cutting garden, as well as for the foreground of the border. A skirt of Lady's-mantle or Missouri Evening Primrose, *Oenothera missouriensis*, will help disguise its gangly legs.

That prime taste maker of the Victorian era, Shirley Hibberd, was enraptured by Balloon Flowers, declaring, "the lover of hardy plants should give no rest to the soles of his feet or the palms of his hands till he has mastered every detail of their cultivation." Fortunately, the basics are pretty simple—Balloon Flowers thrive

OPPOSITE, a tureen holds a cool collection of old-fashioned favourites: Balloon Flower, *Platycodon grandiflorus*, Borage, *Borago officinalis*, and pale lavender spikes of *Hosta sieboldiana*. ABOVE, the buds of *Platycodon grandiflorus* change from green to lavender as they swell before they open; the flowers have been cottage garden favourites since the nineteenth century.

with a minimum of care in a wide diversity of soils. It is best to select a sunny site in moisture-retentive fertile ground. A winter mulch or covering is called for in cold-winter areas. The plants are almost totally free of pests and diseases. The gardener's soles and palms can rest easy.

Ruta graveolens
Rutaceae

RUE

ABOVE LEFT, the Herb-of-grace, *Ruta graveolens*, sets seed in a terraced herb garden paired
with American wild flower *Lobelia syphilitica*. ABOVE RIGHT, the mustard yellow flowers of
Rue, *Ruta graveolens*, further enhance the blue coloration of the finely-cut foliage, which Pliny
the Elder said was eaten by artists in ages past to empower them with the "second sight."

 The ancient Greeks
were a fretful lot.
There were gods to
honour or one risked
dire consequences.
There were spells to
be cast and be caught by. All manner of
venomous beasts roamed the earth, and
they imagined even worse ones at its far
reaches. One plant was considered

amazingly effective to safeguard man—
Ruta graveolens. The smell of the bruised
leaves must have suggested magic powers
from the earliest times. This smell is both
repugnant and fascinating, somewhat fetid,
and for some unknown reason it reminds
me of nuts. In short, it is unique.

Boiled in wine, the seeds were said to
be the antidote to every poison. The leaves
were used as protection from witchcraft.

Pliny related that, "Engravers, Carvers, and
Painters do ordinarily eat Rue alone for to
preserve their eyesight." Beyond ordinary
vision, they believed that Rue bestowed
the power of the second sight. This is
altogether likely in some respects, for large
quantities of Rue are highly toxic, resulting
in neurological disorders, including halluci-
nations. It was used to calm the hysterical,
ease aching joints, and relieve gout. Mixed
with wine and pepper, it was applied to
remove warts; I feel quite certain this
concoction would remove them.

All the magic of Rue came with it to
England, possibly with the Romans, and
most definitely by the fifteenth century.
The church had the task of bringing the
mystical virtues of the herb within the fold
of Christian doctrine. Sprigs of the plant
were used to sprinkle holy water before
the celebration of high mass, and in
exorcisms, and so it became the Herb of
Grace. Shakespeare spoke of the custom:
"There's rue for you; and here's some for
me; we may call it herb of grace o'
Sundays."

When plagues were about, Rue was
carried to ward off infection. The leaves
were spread on the floors of prisons and
law courts to prevent outbreaks of typhus,
known as jail fever. Bewigged judges,
obliged to share the air of their courts
with unsavoury criminals, kept nosegays of
aromatic plants, including Rue, beneath
their benches to sniff as protection. For all
its bitter taste, it was added to peculiarly
flavoured cheese such as is made from
goat's milk, although one doubts that
anything short of transmission fluid could
disguise that taste. The herb came to
symbolize sorrow and repentance, and was

associated with the regretful verb, as in, "I
rue the day I ate that cheese."

Sadly, Herb-of-grace has lost nearly all
of its marvellous qualities, except as a
superb garden plant. The leaves are blue-
green, almost aqua, lacy and fine. The aqua
colour is further enhanced in summer by
mustard-yellow sprays of tiny flowers.
Clumps grow to about two feet (60cm),
and spread to eighteen inches (45cm).
When it is planted with silver Southern-
wood and mauve-flowering thyme, the
muted tones create an illusion of old
tapestry. It is equally lovely in the flower
border with golden yellow *Heliopsis* and
Inula. Although I have never seen it planted
in this manner, I can imagine the subtle
effect of the fine-cut leaves of Rue against
the bold blue ones of *Hosta sieboldiana*.
Gertrude Jekyll combined Rue with
clumps of pale blue *Campanula lactiflora* and
the branches of the white Everlasting Pea,
writing, "In front of this there is a drift of
Rue, giving a beautiful effect of dim grey
colour and softened shadow; it is crowned
by its spreading corymbs of pale yellow
bloom. . . ."

The plants are of simple culture,
needing sun and good drainage. They
thrive in soils where lime is present. Rue is
hardy except in very cold winters, and not
an insect would dare touch it.

Ruta graveolens is one of the few plants
to be represented clearly in heraldry, and is
shown in the Collar of the British Order of
the Thistle. Two old superstitions about
Rue are of value to gardeners. First, it is
reputed to grow best and be the most
potent near a fig tree. Secondly, for Rue to
prosper, it must be stolen. The gardener
must draw his own conclusions.

Santolina chamaecyparissus is yet another herb of the Mediterranean countries that has been grown in England for so long that it is impossible to pinpoint when it arrived. Turner first mentions *Santolina* in 1548, under the names Lavender Cotton and Female Abrotatum. It was certainly grown in Gerard's day, for he wrote, "Lavender Cotton bringeth foorth

clustered buttons of a golden colour and of sweete smell and is often used in garlands and in decking up of gardens and houses. . . ." Its early and continuous popularity was in large part due to its value as an edging plant. Knot gardens, so fashionable in Tudor times, relied heavily on tightly clipped hedges of Lavender Cotton. Parkinson was of the opinion that, "the whole plant is of a strong sweete sent, but not unpleasant, and is in many places planted in Gardens, to border knots with,

for which it will abide to be cut in what forme you think best; for it groweth thick and bushy, very fit for such works. . . ."

Like so many herbs with aromatic smells and bitter tastes, it was at first presumed to have medicinal uses. The name *Santolina* was popularly thought to have been derived from *sancta*, holy, and *linum*, flax, and to mean "holy flax." Or it was taken to be the diminutive of *sancta*, in which case the meaning would be "holy little herb." It was, however, blessed with

Santolina Compositae

Santolina chamaecyparissus
LAVENDER COTTON

Santolina virens
GREEN SANTOLINA

few medicinal virtues, and all attempts at finding any were fruitless, save as an insect repellent. The French called it Garde Robe, as it kept moths from clothes.

The binomial designation *chamaecyparissus* refers to the plant's resemblance to the evergreen tree *Chamaecyparis*, often called false cypress. *Santolina* is of the family Compositae—the daisy tribe—and is not related to cotton in any way, although the leaves do have the texture of fabric, and do take on a lavender tint in the right light. A

species with green foliage, *S. virens*, has been grown since the beginning of the eighteenth century. Its fine leaves are very bright green, accenting its yellow flowers.

Lavender Cotton is still employed as an edging plant, either clipped to a foot (30cm) or so, or left to its own devices, which are very pretty indeed. The stiff stems grow in a rounded mound, and each one is studded with a yellow button less than an inch (2.5cm) across. Left unclipped it grows to two feet (60cm) and opens gracefully in all directions, flowering from top to bottom. The leaves have a pleasant scent, reminiscent of cedar, and may be dried for decoration or for the wardrobe.

Both grey and green species of *Santolina* thrive in well-drained soil in full sun. Like many small-leaved Mediterranean herbs, the plant is well adapted to periods of high temperatures and drought, as the size and colour of the leaves prevent excessive water loss through evaporation. They are also unpalatable to insects and grazing animals. Lavender Cotton is favoured for seaside plantings as it resists salt spray. Mature plants are customarily clipped back in mid-spring to promote bushiness. Once thought to be very tender, *Santolina* has been found by gardeners to be surprisingly hardy where it is provided with sandy soil, and a winter mulch of hay or leaves is helpful. Plants in my herb garden have defied winters with temperatures as low as minus thirty, although they freeze back. Plants grown in milder climates are evergreen, or ever-grey. Plants recovering from a severe winter may bloom later or not at all. New plants are easily propagated from stem cuttings, and take several years to fully mature.

Santolina virens forms a spreading mound of button flowers in a sun-drenched border, ABOVE.
Lavender Cotton, *Santolina chamaecyparissus*, makes an informal edging to *Geranium pratense*
and young dahlia shoots, OPPOSITE.

There are few flowers of such beauty with such an unflattering name as *Scabiosa*. The name recalls exactly the purpose for which it was valued in the past—to treat scabies, a disease caused by a particularly vile mite that burrows under the skin and deposits eggs; the result is almost unbearable itching. Any plant that could help in such cases would naturally have been highly regarded, and species of Scabyas and Skabiose, as it was already called, were cultivated for that purpose in the fifteenth century. John Russell gives the recipe for a medicinal bath for the Duke of Gloucester, in his *Book of Nature*, written abut 1550. *Scabiosa* is an important ingredient, along with Marsh Mallow and Fennel, all steeped in hot water.

Besides its use in relieving skin diseases, *Scabiosa* was considered effective to treat lung diseases, and in its early stages, the plague. Gerard said it was good for snakebite, and considering the vast numbers of plants recommended to cure the non-lethal bites of the snakes of England, we can be sure the herbalists boasted a very high success rate.

The first species to be imported were *S. graminifolia*, low-growing and lavender, in 1683, and *S. ochroleuca*, sulphur yellow, about 1700. That staple of the flower garden, *Scabiosa caucasica*, first came to gardens in 1803, thanks to stock raised by nurseryman George Loddiges of Hackney; the seed sent to him was collected in the Caucasus Mountains. The discovery of the plant is credited to the explorer and Russian ambassador to England, Count

Scabiosa caucasica
Dipsacaceae

PINCUSHION FLOWER

An arrangement in progress, OPPOSITE, features pink *Phlox paniculata*, the mahogany-toned leaves of Beefsteak Plant, *Perilla frutescens*, and Pincushion Flower, *Scabiosa caucasica* in an antique tin box. ABOVE, long wiry stems hold the blossoms of *Scabiosa caucasica* above the leaves, making them an airy addition to the border, as well as an ideal cutting flower.

Apollon Apollosevich Mussin-Puschkin. (He is commemorated by the spring-blooming bulb *Puschkinia scilloides*; it's too bad the name *Scabiosa* couldn't have been traded in for one of his spare ones.) It was promptly dubbed the Pincushion Flower.

The Wedgewood-blue flowers hold a quaint charm, perhaps because they look like satin cushions stuck with pearl-headed pins. An involucre, or collar, of feathery bracts surrounds the circle of "pins," which are really tiny flowers. These tiny flowers open consecutively from the outside rows inward, eventually filling the centre with a fuzz of fine stamens. The blossoms measure three inches (7.5cm) across, and first appear in June.

The leaves are deeply incised, forming a low mound of green up to two feet (60cm) wide. The flowers are held high, on wiry stalks about twenty inches (50cm) long. These long stems add to the value of the flower for cutting. The lovely white form was first grown at the end of the last century, and there are hybrids of various shades of lavender and blue. William Robinson declared *Scabiosa caucasica* "the finest perennial in my garden, it flowers from early summer to late autumn." The delicate blue of the flowers invites its inclusion in a pastiche of pink, mauve, and rose.

Sun-loving Pincushion Flower grows best in neutral or alkaline soils, kept moist in the summer and with no standing water in the winter. They are quite hardy and carefree. They can be grown from seed. Old plants may cease to bloom well and may be lifted, divided, and planted in humus-enriched earth of a gritty nature.

Scabiosa belongs to the Dipsacaceae, a small family which also counts the wool-carding teasel as a member. The primrose-yellow Giant Scabious is now classified as *Cephalaria gigantea*, to the annoyance of many gardeners. This splendid six-foot (1.8m) Siberian native, too rarely seen, was grown as early as 1759.

Sisyrinchium striatum is a curious plant. At first glance, the leaves would indicate it to be an iris, but the flowers are something quite different. There are over a hundred species of the genus *Sisyrinchium*, most of them, native to North and South America. While most of them which are called Blue-eyed grass, have narrow, grassy foliage and blue flowers, *S. striatum* is atypical, having wide, spearlike leaves, and yellow blossoms.

Then there's the name. It is difficult to pronounce, at best, but should sound something like sis-uh-rink-ee-um. I've heard it dozens of ways, so it seems safest to stick with Yellow-eyed Grass. The Latin name may be translated roughly as pig snout, on account of the fondness swine exhibit for the roots—there is very little about this plant that may be described as ordinary.

Yellow-eyed Grass is native to Chile and Argentina, and came to England by 1788. It has never created much of a stir, perhaps hindered by the name, but more likely by the enormous change in gardening fashion shortly after its introduction. It certainly had its devotees, but in the era of the grand and gaudy, Yellow-eyed Grass was considered neither. It survived in the hands of connoisseurs and collectors.

The grey-green leaves form small clumps up to a little more than a foot (30cm) high. The flower stems rise well above the foliage, usually to two feet (60cm) tall, and bear smaller leaves that diminish in size upward. The upper third of the slender stalk bears evenly spaced

Sisyrinchium striatum
Iridaceae

YELLOW-EYED GRASS

rows of flower clusters. The six-petalled blossoms, an inch wide, are straw yellow with a darker eye. The outsides of the petals are striped with brown or purple. (The epithet *striatum* refers to these stripes.)

Yellow-eyed Grass is probably more widely grown today than at any time in its past, which is not saying much. It is fortunate that it is being rediscovered, for there are few flowers of its colour, and fewer still of such distant form. The flower spikes, which might be considered stiff on their own, are effective when contrasted with matting or mounded plants, such as pinks, catmints, and sun roses (helianthemum). It shares with them, too, a need for a sunny location.

The leaf shoot where a flower spike is produced dies after the flowers have faded. The clumps need rich soil and regular fertilization to ensure plentiful blossoms each year. The leaves are evergreen in mild climates, where plants are often divided in late summer. Frequent division, with the plants reset in fresh humus-enriched soil, keeps Yellow-eyed Grass vigorous. Seedlings often volunteer around established clumps. *S. striatum* is generally not considered hardy in northern gardens, although so few American gardeners are familiar with it, that the limits have barely been tested. I have had success, although not on the level of the counties of East Anglia, where it is grown to perfection.

Aside from pig fodder, which hardly seems suitable, *Sisyrinchium* has few uses other than ornamental. The exception is a Hawaiian species, *S. acre*, which is the source of a dye used in a kind of tattooing that is said to be painless. To date, there has not been a clamour for this plant.

The six-petalled flowers of *S. striatum* have a darker eye and delicate brown stripes on the reverse sides of the petals, ILLUSTRATION, OPPOSITE. OPPOSITE, spear-like leaves and stiff stems studded with small flowers are characteristic of Yellow-eyed Grass, *S. striatum*, which is artfully combined with plants of a more rounded habit, including pinks, dianthus, and sun roses, helianthemum. This subtle combination, ABOVE, works so well because the silver leaves and tiny pink blooms of Lamb's Ears, *Stachys byzantina*, serve as a foil for the tiered stems of *S. striatum*.

The current vogue for silver-leaved plants has thrust *Stachys byzantina* into the forefront of the group, as well as the front of many borders. For a plant that nearly disappeared from cultivation, it has had a remarkable comeback. Lamb's Ears, as it is popularly called, survived several fashion revolutions. It first found favour as an edging plant and went through several rounds of this. As late as a hundred years ago, Peter Henderson wrote that Hedge Nettle, as he knew it, was "used to a considerable extent in the formation of white lines for ribbon borders." At almost the exact same time, but from the other side of the Atlantic, Theresa Earle recommended from her Surrey garden, "Not the smallest and dryest garden should be without *Stachys lanata*, a white woolly leaved plant, called Rabbit's Ears by cottage children, and particularly attractive to some people, who throughout life retain the love for something woolly and soft." Only the nomenclature has changed.

Found growing wild from the Caucasus to Persia, this member of the mint family was introduced in 1782. The name *stakhys*, used by Dioscorides, is Greek for "spike," and refers to the plant's manner of flowering. Older books generally list the species as *S. lanata* or later as *S. olympica*. The current binomial, we hope the last, *byzantina*, refers to the plant's coming from Byzantium, the ancient city on the Bosporus, on whose site was built Constantinople, now Istanbul. It is fascinating that the name of one plant so unassuming would weave through thousands of years.

Stachys
Labiatae

Stachys byzantina
LAMB'S EARS

Stachys officinalis
BETONY

As it grew in gardens grand and humble, its distinct leaves earned *Stachys* the nicknames of Jesus Flannel, Woolly Betony, Donkey's Ear, Lamb's Tongue, and Lamb's Ears. (It would be interesting to plant a garden of plants named for animals, featuring Tiger Lilies, Bear's Ears, not to mention Bear's Breeches and Lion's Ear, Goatsbeard, Partridge Feather, Old Gooseneck, and Pigsqueak. Throw in some foxgloves, snapdragons, toadflax, wolfsbane, and cowslips for a garden that could truly be called the Peaceable Kingdom.)

Lamb's Ears' woolly leaves, four to six inches (10–15cm) long, form dense mats spreading to a foot (30cm) or more. In early summer, the flower stems appear, clothed in the same grey wool. The deep pink tubular flowers are set in tiers up the eighteen-inch (45cm) stems. Mrs. Earle noted how good they are for picking, and observed, "When cut, they go on growing in water, as Buttercups and Forget-me-nots do." Some gardeners object to the flowers and cut them off. Although I don't know any such Victorian throwbacks, the nonblooming variety 'Silver Carpet' makes an excellent groundcover.

I count Lamb's Ears among the most valuable of perennials. Drifts run through my garden like silver currents, sometimes disappearing deep in a border behind clumps of blue Flax or the pale yellow of Scotch broom *Cytisus scoparius* 'Moonlight.' The straggly stems of the Poppy Mallow, *Callirhoe involucrata*, thread through the patches of Lamb's Ears, and its cup-like magenta flowers appear even more brilliant against the silver foliage.

Possible combinations are endless, since *S. byzantina* thrives in so many situations, from full sun in sandy soil to wet clay in partial shade. It is extremely drought-resistant; some plants in my curbside planting receive only three or four supplemental waterings during the summer. New plants may be rooted from cuttings, but the easiest method by far is to divide existing clumps with a sharp border spade in spring. Reset a piece, about eight inches (20cm) across, in the same spot, where it will quickly fill in, and transplant the remaining pieces to a new location.

The Wood Betony of Europe, *Stachys officinalis*, is too rarely grown in gardens today. The violet-pink flowers rise on stiff stems above crinkled heart-shaped leaves of dark green. Despite its name, it grows best in sun. Betony had many uses from the earliest days in England, not the least being protection from witchcraft. A cup of Betony tea was reputed to shield the dreamer from nocturnal visits from unfriendly spirits. By day, the user was relieved of earache and hay fever. The modern gardener values the two-foot (60cm) spikes of vivid flowers in June, when they are particularly pretty with species of *Oenothera*, yellow sundrops.

While Lamb's Ears, *Stachys byzantina*, is often considered only for informal plantings in borders or as an edging, this parterre of clipped boxwood encloses its downy flower spikes in an altogether more dressy manner, ABOVE.

The Romans dedicated *Thalictrum* to Bacchus, which should not dissuade gardeners from growing it, and believed that a child laid on a pillow stuffed with the flowers would lead a rich and charmed life. The name is from the Greeks, probably from *thallo*, to grow green or flourish, in allusion to the young shoots. The native English species, *T. minus*, was used in the treatment of jaundice and the plague, although without much proven success.

For all their five hundred years in gardens, the species of *Thalictrum*, commonly known as meadow rue, have received scant attention. As members of the Ranunculaceae, they are closely related to *Clematis*, *Aconitum*, *Helleborus*, and *Anemone*. They are unrelated to *Ruta graveolens*, the true Rue, although there is a slight likeness in the foliage of the plants. Gerard, in his inimitable style, called them Bastard Rhubarbs. In the seventeenth century their status had improved, and they were known aptly as Spanish Tufts or Feathered Columbines. The foliage is similar to the related columbines, properly *Aquilegia*; the species *T. aquilegiifolium* recalls this, and it is popularly called the Columbine Meadow Rue.

The resemblance to columbines is so close, especially in young seedlings, that mixups are inevitable in the garden and in the nursery trade. For several years, no matter which species I ordered, I ended up planting dozens of *T. aquilegiifolium*. Fortunately, it is among the prettiest of the lot, with fluffy panicles of rosy lavender flowers produced on three-foot (90cm) stems in June. This species, native to Europe and western Asia, came to English gardens early in the eighteenth century. It's not surprising that it was a popular border plant in America by the time Peter Henderson published his *Handbook of Plants* in 1890. What is surprising is that it was the vogue to grow *Thalictrum* solely for its leaves, "which are pretty enough to pass, when mingled with cut flowers, for some of the finer species of Maidenhair Ferns..... For this purpose, the flower stems, which appear in May and June, should be pinched off to encourage the growth of the leaves."

Despite the fern fixation of the late Victorians, this illustrates that the foliage of the meadow rues is attractive throughout the season. No passengers here—in or out of bloom, the plants carry their weight in the border. *T. speciosissimum*, tongue twister though it may be, sports handsome blue-green leaves that in midsummer are topped by flower heads the colour of lemon drops. This stately plant, called the Dusty Meadow Rue, grows to five feet (1.5m), and arrived from Spain and North Africa at the beginning of the eighteenth century. Beware the confusion of names here, for some consider *T. speciosissimum* a subspecies of *T. flavum*. This botanical quandary need not worry gardeners, except that the latter has ordinary green leaves, which spoil the effect of the blue

ILLUSTRATION, TOP, *T. aquilegifolium*. The flower heads of *T. aquilegifolium*, ABOVE RIGHT, impart texture to a wild garden. *T. speciosissimum* has blue-gray foliage, RIGHT.

Thalictrum **Ranunculaceae**

Thalictrum aquilegiifolium COLUMBINE MEADOW RUE

Thalictrum delavayi YUNNAN MEADOW RUE

Thalictrum speciosissimum DUSTY MEADOW RUE

and yellow contrast. The form with the grey foliage is sometimes listed by nurserymen as *T. flavum* 'Glaucum'. (Botanists agree with gardeners here—*flavum* merely means "yellow," while *speciosissimum* means "very showy.")

T. delavayi, Yunnan Meadow Rue, is arguably the finest of the meadow rues. It was discovered in western China by Abbé

pale yellow stamens highlights the tiny mauve flowers. Blooming in mid- and late summer, the stems grow to five feet (1.5m). Graham Stuart Thomas recommends them for cutting, but warns that plants should be spaced several feet apart, "because the flower stalks get entangled and make one say *Cardamine!* or *Damnacanthus!*; they are impossible to separate, but of course help

a true *T. dipterocarpum*, although it is rarely seen. Just to confuse matters further, the species *T. rochebrunianum*—none of these are easy to pronounce—also masquerades by either name. I got it quite by accident and I'm tempted to call it my favourite, for as each species blooms successively, I'm quite taken in by their charms. *T. rochebrunianum* is, thankfully, called Lavender Mist. A dedicated gardener with excellent soil can coax it to grow up to ten feet (3m), but Lavender Mist most often reaches five to seven feet (1.5–2.1m). It bears masses of rosy lavender flowers with fuzzy yellow stamens in late summer and early autumn.

Whether the gardener ends up with the species of meadow rue that he originally had in mind, it's doubtful that he would have cause for complaint unless there isn't room for more than a few dozen Columbine Meadow Rue (which, incidentally, is very pretty massed in front of yellow Trumpet Lilies). The fuzzy yellow flowers of Dusty Meadow Rue are superb planted in conjunction with Monkshood and Lady's Mantle. Despite their height, neither *T. delavayi*, Yunnan Meadow Rue, nor Lavender Mist, *T. rochebrunianum*, need always be relegated to the background. The see-through sprays of flowers provide a delicate focal point among ferns and Japanese Anemones.

ABOVE, sprays of **Yunnan Meadow Rue**, *T. delavayi*, display tufts of cream-coloured stamens in loose, airy panicles. The ray florets of *T. aquilegifolium* give the flowers a fluffy appearance, OPPOSITE.

Delavay and introduced in 1890. The plant is elegant and ethereal, with an elongated pyramid of flowers above fine foliage. The flowers are not packed into dense heads, but dangle from loose branches. A tuft of

to hold each other in place in the garden."

Lovely as *T. delavayi* is, its name is the most confused, rendering this a difficult plant to purchase. It is most often called *T. dipterocarpum* in gardens, but there really is

Meadow rues are of the easiest culture, thriving in sun or light shade in all types of soil. They do best with average moisture, but will tolerate even soggy ground. They are hardy almost everywhere. Under favourable conditions, they may volunteer look-alike seedlings, which are easily transplanted.

The Calla Lily calls to mind many associations, perhaps of glamorous living, stylish flower shops, or in my case, Katharine Hepburn. One of the most imitated lines of the century must be of the great actress in *Stage Door*, when with a single flower in her hands, she walks through the terrace door of a set, intoning with that voice, "The Calla Lilies are in bloom again. . . ."

Few of us associate the Calla Lily, properly *Zantedeschia aethiopica*, with Africa. Nevertheless, the flower we imagine as a hothouse rarity of elegance and refinement grows with wild abandon throughout southern Africa. From May until December, especially near Cape Town, every ditch and stream, every moist meadow, glows with the ivory spathes.

Imagine the excitement of early explorers who discovered the plants, and the fuss back home in 1731, when the Callas were introduced. They are also called Lily of the Nile and Arum Lilies, although they don't grow on the Nile, and they are neither arums nor lilies. *Zantedeschia* is a member of the Araceae, an exotic family which includes *Anthurium, Caladium*, two genera of famous houseplants—*Philodendron* and *Monstera*—and *Symplocarpus foetidus*, the infamous Skunk Cabbage of North America. They are also related to the bog plants of the genus *Calla*, with which they were originally confused. The botanical name honours Francesco Zantedeschi, an Italian botanist who died in 1873, although old books list them as *Richardia africana*.

Early settlers in the Cape region considered them a roadside weed and referred to them as Pig Lilies, since porcupines, which they called pigs, eat the fleshy roots. A tale is told of a rich merchant who commissioned a fashionable London floral designer to create the arrangements for his daughter's wedding. The boxes were shipped at great expense to Cape Town, and when opened, revealed bouquets of Pig Lilies.

The unusual flowers grow above glossy green arrow-shaped leaves, and are carried on thick, stiff stems up to two feet (60cm) long. Each consists of a yellow spike, called a spadix, crowded with tiny inconspicuous true flowers, which is enfolded by the white trumpet, called a spathe. It is the graceful curve of the spathe, five to ten inches (12.5–23cm) long, that has long fascinated florists, artists, and gardeners.

The Calla Lily is hardy in many parts of the British Isles, as well as in mild-winter states such as California. It is a traditional flower in cities of the Old South, such as New Orleans, where it grows luxuriantly in partial shade. In the mild regions where they can be grown outdoors permanently,

BELOW, a variety of *Zantedeschia aethiopica* known as 'Crowborough' has proved to be the hardiest of the South African Calla Lily. The curved spathes of Calla Lilies need little else to make an elegant arrangement, OPPOSITE.

Calla Lilies grow robustly in deep, rich soil with abundant moisture. Sunny positions are preferable in cooler maritime climates, but the plants need some shade in warmer southern gardens. They are at home at pondside, and in areas where they are marginally hardy, may survive planted in deep mud in a pool, where frost does not reach below the freezing line to their deep-delving roots. Positioning plants near south-facing walls may also see them through the winter. The variety 'Crowborough' is a selection found growing in an open sunny border in a Sussex garden, and has proved to be hardier and less thirsty. New plants should be heavily mulched for the first few years, and thereafter as a precaution.

In colder areas, it is possible to grow *Z. aethiopica* outdoors in pots in summer and protect the plants in winter. To grow Calla Lilies in containers outside, plant the tubers in spring, setting them vertically in large pots with the bud-end up. The tips should be level with the soil surface, and the potting mixture should be a rich loam. Water moderately at first, until the leaves begin to show, and then top-dress the soil with several inches of compost and rich soil, and keep moist. Regular fertilization will enhance blooming, and protection from afternoon sun is necessary. The plants may be brought indoors in the autumn and will stay green, although normally water is gradually withheld, so as to imitate the dry season of their homeland, where the tubers go dormant.

Arrangers often go hog wild, so to speak, with Calla Lilies—probably less so in Africa—although a few graceful stems of flowers are a bouquet in themselves.

Zantedeschia aethiopica
Araceae

CALLA LILY

SOURCES

WHERE TO FIND
THE FLOWERS

The addresses for the nurseries noted below are listed alphabetically beginning on page 152.

Acanthus mollis
WIDELY AVAILABLE.

Acanthus spinosus
WIDELY AVAILABLE.

Achillea filipendulina
STILLINGFLEET LODGE NURSERIES; WATERPERRY HORTICULTURAL CENTRE; WINTERGREEN NURSERIES.

Achillea millefolium
GLEBE COTTAGE PLANTS; HOLLINGTON NURSERIES; IDEN CROFT HERBS; NETHERFIELD HERBS; NPK LANDLIFE; SELLET HALL HERBS.

Achillea ptarmica 'The Pearl'
WIDELY AVAILABLE.

Aconitum napellus

BERGOVER PLANTS; HADSPEN GARDEN AND
NURSERY; OLD COURT NURSERIES; POYNTZFIELD
HERB NURSERY; ROWDEN GARDENS; SELLET
HALL HERBS; SHEPTON NURSERY GARDEN;
SIFELLE NURSERY; STILLINGFLEET LODGE
NURSERIES; STONE HOUSE COTTAGE NURSERIES.

Alchemilla mollis

WIDELY AVAILABLE.

Alchemilla vulgaris

DAPHNE FFISKE HERBS; OAK COTTAGE HERB
FARM; POYNTZFIELD HERB NURSERY; STOKE
LACY HERB GARDENS.

Allium cernuum

WIDELY AVAILABLE.

Allium christophii

AVON BULBS; BREGOVER PLANTS; CAMBRIDGE
BULBS; GLEBE COTTAGE PLANTS; HADSPEN
GARDEN AND NURSERY; HILLVIEW HARDY
PLANTS; INGWERSEN; JACQUES AMAND;
RAVENINGHAM HALL GARDENS; RUSHFIELDS OF
LEDBURY; STILLINGFLEET LODGE NURSERIES;
UNUSUAL PLANTS; WALTER BLOM.

Allium senescens

CAMBRIDGE BULBS; CHARTER HOUSE NURSERY;
HOLDEN CLOUGH NURSERY; ROGER POULETT.

Allium tuberosum

BULLWOOD NURSERY; CHESHIRE HERBS; IDEN
CROFT HERBS; POYNTZFIELD HERB NURSERY;
SELLET HALL HERBS; THE SMALL NURSERY.

Alstroemeria aurantiaca

BRIDGEMERE NURSERIES; GLEBE COTTAGE PLANTS; LANGTHORNS PLANTERY; MARWOOD HILL GARDENS; PERRYHILL NURSERIES.

Alstroemeria ligtu

WIDELY AVAILABLE.

Althaea officinalis

CHESHIRE HERBS; DAPHNE FFISKE HERBS; HOLLINGTON NURSERIES; IDEN CROFT HERBS; KINGSFIELD TREE NURSERY; LANGTHORNS PLANTERY; NETHERFIELD HERBS; OAK COTTAGE HERB FARM; PLANTS FROM A COUNTRY GARDEN; POLYPHANT HERB GARDEN; POYNTZFIELD HERB NURSERY; SELLET HALL HERBS; SIFELLE NURSERY; STOKE LACY HERB GARDEN; THE HANNAYS OF BATH.

Astrantia major

WIDELY AVAILABLE.

Belamcanda chinensis

HOO HOUSE NURSERY; HOPLEYS PLANTS; THE OLD MANOR NURSERY; TOWN FARM NURSERY; TREASURES OF TENBURY; UNUSUAL PLANTS; M.C. WICKENDEN.

Bergenia cordifolia

WIDELY AVAILABLE.

Campanula carpatica

ABBOTS HOUSE GARDEN; CHARTER HOUSE NURSERY; COTON MANOR GARDEN; GLEBE COTTAGE PLANTS; GLENVIEW ALPINE NURSERY; HIGHGATES NURSERY; HILLVIEW HARDY PLANTS; HOO HOUSE NURSERY; JACK DRAKE; KIFTSGATE COURT GARDENS; NORTHUMBRIA NURSERIES; PADLOCK CROFT; ROOKHOPE NURSERIES; SHEPTON NURSERY GARDEN; WINGWELL NURSERY; WINTERGREEN NURSERIES.

Campanula persicifolia

WIDELY AVAILABLE.

Campanula poscharskyana

BALLALHEANNAGH GARDENS; BUCKINGHAM NURSERIES; BURNLOOSE & SOUTH DOWN NURSERIES; CASTLE ALPINES; DAISY HILL NURSERIES; DAVID AUSTIN; ELWORTHY COTTAGE GARDEN PLANTS; GLENVIEW ALPINE NURSERY; HIGHLAND LILIUMS; PETER TRENEAR; RAMPARTS NURSERIES; REGINALD KAYE; THE MARGERY FISH NURSERY; TREASURES OF TENBURY.

Campanula punctata

BLACKTHORN NURSERY; CHARTER HOUSE NURSERY; ELWOTHY COTTAGE GARDEN PLANTS; PADLOCK CROFT; PLANTS FROM A COUNTRY GARDEN; PLANTS FROM THE PAST; SIFELLE NURSERY; THE OLD MANOR NURSERY; TREASURES OF TENBY; WASHFIELD NURSERY.

Campanula rotundifolia

GLEBE COTTAGE PLANTS; JOHN CLAYFIELD; OAK COTTAGE HERB FARM; PADLOCK CROFT; PLANTS FROM A COUNTRY GARDEN; ROOKHOPE NURSERIES; SIFELLE NURSERY; SOUTHFARTHING ALPINES; TREASURES OF TENBURY.

Campsis radicans

CHURCHILLS GARDEN NURSERY; HILLIER NURSERIES; KNAPHILL & SLOCOCK; NOTTCUTTS NURSERIES; PERRYHILL NURSERIES; ROYAL HORTICULTURAL GARDEN; STONE HOUSE COTTAGE NURSERIES; WATERPERRY HORTICULTURAL CENTRE.

Centranthus ruber

CHESHIRE HERBS; PLANTS FROM A COUNTRY GARDEN; SELLET HALL HERBS; TREASURES OF TENBURY; WINGWELL NURSERY.

Clematis davidiana

FISK'S CLEMATIS NURSERY; PEVERIL CLEMATIS NURSERY; TREASURES OF TENBURY.

Clematis integrifolia

FISK'S CLEMATIS NURSERY; PEVERIL CLEMATIS NURSERY; TREASURES OF TENBURY.

Clematis recta

FISK'S CLEMATIS NURSERY; PEVERIL CLEMATIS NURSERY; TREASURES OF TENBURY.

Crucianella stylosa

BOSVIGO PLANTS; GLENVIEW ALPINE NURSERY; HADSPEN GARDEN & NURSERY; HOLDEN CLOUGH NURSERY; UNUSUAL PLANTS.

Erigeron karvinskianus

BRIDGEMERE NURSERIES; DAISY HILL NURSERIES; EASTGROVE COTTAGE GARDEN NURSERY; GREAT DIXTER NURSERIES; REGINALD KAYE.

Erigeron speciosus

HILLVIEW HARDY PLANTS; NORDEN ALPINES; RUSHFIELDS OF LEDBURY.

Eryngium alpinium

BRIDGEMERE NURSERIES; HILLIER NURSERIES; JACK DRAKE; SAVILL GARDENS; TREASURES OF TENBURY; UNUSUAL PLANTS.

Eryngium giganteum

WIDELY AVAILABLE.

Eryngium planum

WIDELY AVAILABLE.

Gentiana lutea

HOLLINGTON NURSERIES; IDEN CROFT HERBS; UNUSUAL PLANTS.

Geranium endressii

WIDELY AVAILABLE.

Geranium pratense

COTON NURSERIES; JOHN CLAYFIELD; SIFELLE NURSERY; THE MARGERY FISH NURSERY; TOAD HALL PRODUCE.

Geranium psilostemon

WIDELY AVAILABLE.

Geranium sanguineum

WIDELY AVAILABLE.

Gunnera manicata

WIDELY AVAILABLE.

Heracleum mantegazzianum

BRIDGEMERE NURSERIES; OAK COTTAGE HERB FARM; RAVENINGHAM HALL GARDENS; ROWDEN GARDENS.

Hosta sieboldiana

WIDELY AVAILABLE.

Hypericum calycinum

WIDELY AVAILABLE.

Iris pseudacorus

AVON BULBS; DAVID AUSTIN; HADSPEN GARDEN & NURSERY; HOLLINGTON NURSERIES; HONEYSOME AQUATIC NURSERY; MAYDENCROFT AQUATIC NURSERIES; NORTHUMBRIA NURSERIES; ROWDEN GARDENS; STAPELEY WATER GARDENS; THE WATER GARDEN NURSERY; WINTERGREEN NURSERIES.

Iris versicolor

BLAGDON WATER GARDEN CENTRE; HONEYSOME AQUATIC NURSERY; MAYDENCROFT AQUATIC NURSERIES; NPK LANDLIFE; PARADISE CENTRE; STAPELEY WATER GARDENS.

Kniphofia uvaria

BLOOMS OF BRESSINGHAM; HADSPEN GARDEN & NURSERY; LANGTHORNS PLANTERY; SHEPTON NURSERY GARDEN; WINGWELL NURSERY.

Lavandula angustifolia

ABERCONWY NURSERY; HILLIER NURSERIES; NOTCUTTS NURSERIES; PLANTS FROM A COUNTRY GARDEN; POYNTZFIELD HERB NURSERY; SELLET HALL HERBS; THE MARGERY FISH NURSERY.

Lilium candidum

LANGTHORNS PLANTERY; WALTER BLOM.

Lilium hansonii

JACQUES AMAND; WALTER BLOM.

Lilium martagon

AVON BULBS; BALLALHEANNAGH GARDENS; JACQUES AMAND; LANGTHORNS PLANTERY.

Lychnis chalcedonica

WIDELY AVAILABLE.

Lychnis coronaria

WIDELY AVAILABLE.

Lysimachia clethroides

WIDELY AVAILABLE.

Lysimachia punctata

WIDELY AVAILABLE.

Malva alcea

ROOKHOPE NURSERIES; SHEPTON NURSERY GARDEN.

Nepeta cataria

CHESHIRE HERBS; DAPHNE FFISKE HERBS; HOLLINGTON NURSERIES; IDEN CROFT HERBS; NETHERFIELD HERBS; POYNTZFIELD HERB NURSERY; SELLET HALL HERBS; THE MARGERY FISH NURSERY.

Nepeta x faassenii

BRIDGEMERE NURSERIES; BUCKINGHAM NURSERIES; HILLIER NURSERIES; REGINALD KAYE; TREASURES OF TENBURY.

Nepeta siberica

EASTGROVE COTTAGE GARDEN NURSERY; STILLINGFLEET LODGE NURSERIES; UNUSUAL PLANTS.

Origanum dictamnus

HOPLEYS PLANTS; ROGER POULETT; SIFELLE NURSERY; THE FORTESCUE GARDEN TRUST; THE OLD MANOR NURSERY; M.C. WICKENDEN.

Origanum vulgare

CHESHIRE HERBS; COTON MANOR GARDEN; EASTGROVE COTTAGE GARDEN NURSERY; HOLLINGTON NURSERIES; NETHERFIELD HERBS; POLYPHANT HERB GARDEN; POYNTZFIELD HERB NURSERY; SELLET HALL HERBS; STOKE LACY HERB GARDENS; THE MARGERY FISH NURSERY.

Phygelius capensis

WIDELY AVAILABLE.

Platycodon grandiflorus

GLEBE COTTAGE PLANTS; GREAT DIXTER
NURSERIES; HADSPEN GARDEN & NURSERY; HOO
HOUSE NURSERY; INGWERSEN; JOHN CLAYFIELD;
NORTHUMBRIA NURSERIES; REGINALD KAYE;
UNUSUAL PLANTS.

Ruta graveolens

BRIDGEMERE NURSERIES; CHESHIRE HERBS;
EASTGROVE COTTAGE GARDEN NURSERY; GLEBE
COTTAGE PLANTS; HOLLINGTON NURSERIES;
IDEN CROFT HERBS; SELLET HALL HERBS;
UNUSUAL PLANTS.

Santolina chamaecyparissus

WIDELY AVAILABLE.

Santolina virens

WIDELY AVAILABLE.

Scabiosa caucasica

ABBOTS HOUSE GARDEN; BLACKTHORN
NURSERY; BROADSTONE ALPINES; HIGHLAND
LILIUMS; OLD COURT NURSERIES; PLANTS FROM
A COUNTRY GARDEN; WINTERGREEN
NURSERIES.

Sisyrinchium striatum

WIDELY AVAILABLE.

Stachys byzantina

WIDELY AVAILABLE.

Stachys officinalis

DAPHNE FFISKE HERBS; IDEN CROFT HERBS;
INGWERSEN; JOHN CLAYFIELD; NETHERFIELD
HERBS; STOKE LACY HERB GARDENS; WINGWELL
NURSERY.

Thalictrum aquilegifolium

WIDELY AVAILABLE.

Thalictrum delavayi

WIDELY AVAILABLE.

Thalictrum speciosissimum

BLACKTHORN NURSERY; CHURCHILLS GARDEN
NURSERY; DAVID AUSTIN; EASTGROVE COTTAGE
GARDEN NURSERY; LANGTHORNS PLANTERY;
OAK COTTAGE HERB FARM; OLD COURT
NURSERIES; PLANTS FROM A COUNTRY GARDEN;
SHEPTON NURSERY GARDEN; SIFELLE NURSERY;
TREASURES OF TENBURY; UNUSUAL PLANTS;
WINTERGREEN NURSERIES.

Zantedeschia aethiopica

AVON BULBS; EASTGROVE COTTAGE GARDEN
NURSERY; GREAT DIXTER NURSERIES; HADSPEN
GARDEN & NURSERY; HONEYSOME AQUATIC
NURSERY; JACQUES AMAND; MAYDENCROFT
AQUATIC NURSERIES; STAPELEY WATER
GARDENS; THE WATER GARDEN NURSERY;
TREASURES OF TENBURY; M.C. WICKENDEN.

Abbots House Garden
10 High Street
Abbot's Langley
Herts WD5 OAR

Aberconwy Nursery
Craig, Glan Conwy
Colwyn Bay
Clwyd LL28 7TL

Avon Bulbs
Upper Westwood
Bradford-on-Avon
Wilts BA15 2AT

Ballalheannagh Gardens
Glen Roy, Lonan
Isle of Man

Blagdon Water Garden Centre
Bath Road, Upper Langford
Avon BS18 7DN

Blooms of Bressingham
Diss
Norfolk IP22 2AB

Bosvigo Plants
Bosvigo House
Bosvigo Lane, Truro
Cornwall TR1 3NH

Bregover Plants
Hillbrooke, Middlewood
North Hill, Launceston
Cornwall PL15 7NN

Bridgemere Nurseries
Bridgemere
Cheshire CW5 7QB

Broadstone Alpines
13 The Nursery
High Street, Sutton Courtnay
Oxfordshire OX14 4UA

Buckingham Nurseries
14 Tingewick Road
Buckingham
Bucks MK18 4AE

Bullwood Nursery
54 Woodlands Road
Hockley
Essex SS5 4PY

Burncoose & South Down Nurseries
Gwennap
Redruth
Cornwall TR16 6BJ

NURSERIES

Cambridge Bulbs
40 Whittlesford Road
Newton
Cambs CB2 5PH

Castle Alpines
Castle Road
Wotton, Woodstock
Oxfordshire, OX7 1EG

Charter House Nursery
Charter House
Trogneer Road
Dumfriesshire DG2 7RE

Cheshire Herbs
Fourfields
Forest Road, Little Budworth
Cheshire CW6 9ES

Churchills Garden Nursery
Exeter Road
Chudleigh
Devon TQ13 ODD

Coton Manor Garden
Guilsborough
Northampton NN6 8RQ

Coton Nurseries
Brook Lane, Coton
Cambridge CB3 7PY

Daisy Hill Nurseries
Hospital Road
Newry, Co. Down
N. Ireland BT35 8PN

Daphne Ffiske Herbs
Rosemary Cottage
Bramerton, Norwich
Norfolk NR14 7DW

David Austin
Bowling Green Lane
Albrighton
Wolverhampton WV7 3HB

Eastgrove Cottage Garden Nursery
Sankyns Green
nr. Shrawley, Little Witley
Worcs WR6 6LQ

Elworthy Cottage Garden Plants
Elworthy
Taunton, Somerset TA4 3PX

Fisk's Clematis Nursery
Westleton
Saxmundham
Suffolk IP17 3AJ

Glebe Cottage Plants
Pixie Lane
Warkleigh, Umberleigh
Devon EX37 9DH

Glenview Alpine Nursery
Quarry Hill, by Forfar
Angus
Tayside DD8 3TQ

Great Dixter Nurseries
Northiam, Rye
East Sussex TN31 6PH

Hadspen Garden and Nursery
Castle Cary
Somerset BA7 7NG

Highgates Nursery
166a Crich Lane
Belper
Derbyshire DE5 1EP

Highland Liliums
Kiltarlity-by-Beauly
Inverness IV4 7JQ

Hillier Nurseries
Ampfield House, Ampfield
Hants SO51 9PA

Hillview Hardy Plants
Worfield
Bridgenorth
Shropshire WV15 5NT

Holden Clough Nursery
Holden, Bolton-by-Bowland
Clitheroe
Lancs BB7 4PF

Hollington Nurseries
Woolton Hill
Newbury
Berks RG15 9XT

Honeysome Aquatic Nursery
The Row, Sutton, nr. Ely
Cambridge, CB6 2PF

Hoo House Nursery
Hoo House, Gloucester Road
Tewkesbury
Gloucester GL20 7DA

Hopleys Plants
High Street
Much Hadham
Herts SG10 6BU

Iden Croft Herbs
Frittenden Road
Staplehurst
Kent TN12 ODH

W.E.Th. Ingwersen
Birch Farm Nursery
Gravetye, East Grinstead
West Sussex RH19 4LE

Jack Drake
Inshriach Alpine Nursery
Aviemore
Inverness PH22 IQS

Jacques Amand
The Nurseries
Clamp Hill, Stanmore
Middlesex, HA7 3JS

John Clayfield
16 Bernards Hill
Bridgenorth
Shropshire WV15 5AX

Kiftsgate Court Gardens
Kiftsgate Court
Chipping Camden
Gloucestershire

Knaphill & Slocock Nurseries
Barrs Lane
Knaphill, Woking
Surrey GU21 2JW

Langthorns Plantery
High Cross Lane West
Little Canfield, Dunmow
Essex CM6 1TD

Marwood Hill Gardens
Barnstaple
Devon EX31 4EB

Maydencroft Aquatic Nurseries
Maydencroft Lane
Gosmore, Hitchin
Herts SG4 7QD

NPK Landlife
542 Parrs Wood Road
East Didsbury
Manchester M20 OQA

Norden Alpines
2 Meadowcroft
Low Street Carlton, nr. Goole
N. Humberside DN14 9PH

Northumbria Nurseries
Castle Gardens, Ford
Berwick-upon-Tweed
Northumberland TD15 2PZ

Notcutts Nurseries
Woodbridge
Suffolk IP12 4AF

Oak Cottage Herb Farm
Nesscliffe
nr. Shrewsbury
Shropshire SY4 1DB

Old Court Nurseries
Colwall
Malvern
Worcs WR13 6QE

Padlock Croft
19 Padlock Road
West Wratting
Cambridge CB1 5LS

Paradise Centre
Twinstead Road
Lamarsh, Bures
Suffolk CO8 5EX

Perryhill Nurseries
Hartfield
Sussex TN7 4JP

Peter Trenear
Chantreyland
Chequers Lane, Eversley Cross
Hants RG27 ONX

Plants From A Country Garden
The Thatched Cottage
Duck Lane, Ludgershall
Aylesbury, Bucks HP18 9NZ

Plants From The Past
The Old House
1 North Street, Belhaven
Dunbar EH42 1NU

Polyphant Herb Garden
Polyphant
Launceston
Cornwall PL15 7PS

Poyntzfield Herb Nursery
Black Isle, Dingwell
Ross and Cromarty
Scotland IV7 8LX

Ramparts Nursery
Hempster Farm
Combe Martin
Devon EX34 ONY

Raveningham Hall Gardens
Norwich
Norfolk NR14 6NS

Reginald Kaye
Waithman Nurseries
Silverdale, Carnforth
Lancs LA5 OTY

Roger Poulett
Nurse's Cottage
North Mundham, Chichester
Sussex PO20 6JY

Rookhope Nurseries
Rookhope, Upper Weardale
Durham DL13 2DD

Rowden Gardens
Brentor, nr. Tavistock
Devon PL19 ONG

Royal Horticultural Garden
Rosemoor, Great Torrington
Devon EX38 8PH

Rushfields of Ledbury
Ross Road, Ledbury
Hereford HR8 2LP

Savill Gardens
Crown Estate Office
The Great Park, Windsor
Berks SL4 2HT

Sellet Hall Herbs
Whittington, via Carnforth
Lancs LA6 2QF

Shepton Nursery Garden
Old Wells Road
Shepton Mallet
Somerset BA4 5XN

Sifelle Nursery
The Walled Garden
Newick Park
Newick, Sussex

Southfarthing Alpines
Southfarthing
Hawkenbury, Staplehurst
Kent TN12 OEP

Stapeley Water Gardens
London Road, Stapeley
Cheshire CW5 7LH

Stillingfleet Lodge Nurseries
Stillingfleet
Yorks YO4 6HW

Stoke Lacy Herb Gardens
Bromyard
Hereford HR7 4JH

Stone House Cottage Nurseries
Stone, nr. Kidderminster
Worcs DY10 4BG

The Hannays of Bath
Sydney Wharf Nursery
Bathwick, Bath
Avon BA2 4ES

The Margery Fish Nursery
East Lambrook Manor
East Lambrook, South Petherton
Somerset TA13 5HL

The Old Manor Nursery
Twyning
Gloucestershire GL20 6DB

The Small Nursery
The Lodge
Aymestry School, Crown East
Worcester WR2 5TR

The Water Garden Nursery
Highcroft, Moorend
Chumleigh
Devon EX18 7SG

Toad Hall Produce
Frogmore, Weston-under-Penyard
Herefordshire

Town Farm Nursery
Whitton
Stillington, Stockton-on-Tees
Cleveland TS21 ILQ

Treasures of Tenbury
Burford House Gardens
Tenbury Wells
Worcs WR15 8HQ

Unusual Plants
Beth Chatto Gardens
Elmstead Market, Colchester
Essex CO7 7DB

Walter Blom
Coombelands Nurseries
Leavesden, Watford
Herts WD2 7BH

Washfield Nursery
Horn's Road
Hawkhurst
Kent TN18 4QU

Waterperry Horticultural Centre
nr. Wheatley
Oxfordshire OX9 1JZ

M.C. Wickenden
Cally Gardens
Gatehouse of Fleet
Castle Douglas, Scotland DG7 2DJ

Wingwell Nursery
Top Street
Wing, Oakham
Leics LE15 8SE

Wintergreen Nurseries
Bringsty Common
Worcs WR6 5UW

Anderson, A. W. 1945. *How We Got Our Flowers.* New York: Dover.

Baumann, Hellmut. 1984. *Le Bouquet d'Athéna.* Paris: La Maison Rustique.

Baynard, Tania. 1985. *Sweet Herbs and Sundry Flowers.* New York: The Metropolitan Museum of Art.

Breck, Joseph. 1851. *The Flower Garden.* Boston: J. P. Jewett. Facsimile edition 1988. Guilford, CT: OPUS Publications.

Chatto, Beth. 1989. *The Green Tapestry.* London: Collins.

Coats, Alice M. 1956. *Flowers and Their Histories.* London: Hulton Press, Ltd.

Davis, P. H., ed. 1978. *Flora of Turkey and the East Aegean Islands.* Edinburgh: Edinburgh University Press.

Dorrance, Anne. 1945. *Green Cargoes.* Garden City, NY: Doubleday, Doran, and Co.

Everett, Thomas H. 1981. *The New York Botanical Garden Illustrated Encyclopedia of Horticulture.* New York: Garland Publishing, Inc.

Ewart, Neil. 1982. *The Lore of Flowers.* Poole, Dorset: Blandford Press.

Favretti, Rudy J. and Joy Putnam. 1978. *Landscapes and Gardens for Historic Buildings.* Nashville: American Association for State and Local History.

Fish, Margery. 1980. *Cottage Garden Flowers.* London: Faber and Faber.

Fisher, John. 1982. *The Origin of Garden Plants.* London: Constable.

BIBLIOGRAPHY

Fogg, H. G. Witham. 1976. *History of Popular Garden Plants from A to Z.* London: Kaye and Ward; New York: A. S. Barnes & Co.

Genders, Roy. 1983. *The Cottage Garden and the Old-Fashioned Flowers.* London: Pelham Books Ltd. Second edition.

————. 1975. *Growing Old Fashioned Flowers.* New York: A. S. Barnes and Co.

Gorer, Richard. 1975. *The Flower Garden in England.* London: B.T. Batsford Ltd.

Gorkin, Nancy Kline, ed. 1989. *Perennials: A Nursery Source Manual.* New York: Brooklyn Botanic Garden, Inc. Vol. 44, No. 4 of Plants and Gardens, Brooklyn Botanic Garden Record.

Grierson, Mary. 1988. *An English Florilegium.* New York: Abbeville Press.

Haughton, Claire Shaver. 1978. *Green Immigrants.* New York: Haughton Harcourt Brace Jovanovich.

Henderson, Peter. 1890. *Henderson's Handbook of Plants and General Horticulture.* New York: P. Henderson & Co.

Huxley, Anthony. 1978. *An Illustrated History of Gardening.* London and New York: Paddington Press.

Ingwerson, Will. 1975. *Classic Garden Plants.* Feltham, England: Collingridge.

Jekyll, Gertrude. 1983. *Color Schemes for the Flower Garden.* Salem, NH: The Ayer Co.

Krutch, Joseph Wood. 1976. *Herbal.* Boston: David R. Godine.

Lehner, Ernst and Johanna. 1960. *Folklore and Symbolism of Flowers, Plants and Trees.* New York: Tudor.

MacFadyen, David. 1982. *A Cottage Flora.* Exeter: Webb and Bower.

Perry, Frances. 1972. *Flowers of the World.* London: Hamlyn.

Rose, Jeanne. 1975. *Herbs & Things.* New York: Grosset & Dunlap Workman Publishing Co.

Shishkin, B. K., ed. 1957. *Flora of the U.S.S.R.* Moscow: Akadamiya Nauk SSSR, translated from Russian by Israel Program for Scientific Translation, 1972.

Stuart, David and Sutherland, James. 1987. *Plants from the Past.* Harmondsworth: Viking.

Synge, Patrick M. 1980. *Lilies: A Revision of Elwes' Monograph of the Genus Lilium and its Supplements.* London: Batsford.

Taylor, Raymond L. 1952. *Plants of Colonial Days.* Williamsburg: Colonial Williamsburg Press.

Thomas, Graham Stuart. 1982. *Perennial Garden Plants, or The Modern Florilegium.* London: J. M. Dent & Sons Ltd.

Whitten, Faith and Geoff. 1985. *Making a Cottage Garden.* London: Bell and Hyman.

INDEX

Page numbers in italic indicate illustrations

Call of the Orient

CHINESE
Cooking

Published 2008 by
Prakash Books India Pvt. Ltd.
1, Ansari Road, Daryaganj
New Delhi 110 002, India.
E-mail: sales@prakashbooks.com
Website: www.prakashbooks.com
Tel: 91-11-23247062-65

ISBN: 978-81-7234-264-7

Printed & bound in India at: Presstech Litho Pvt. Ltd.

Call of the Orient

CHINESE
Cooking

Inspired by STAR TV Shows

Contents

Introduction

If there is any cuisine that has spread its wings all over the world, it is Chinese food. Found in almost all places, the cuisine has a varied base owing to the fact that the national cuisine comes from eight different regions, namely, Anhui, Cantonese, Fujian, Hunan, Jiangsu, Shandong, Szechuan and Zhejiang. It also draws heavily from Buddhist and Muslim sub-cuisines.

A Chinese meal typically consists of two courses. Their main dish is all carbohydrates, mainly rice based dishes and the meats and vegetables are considered accompaniments. This is a departure from the European style where meat is generally taken to be the main course.

Rice is undoubtedly the most important component of Chinese food. However, exceptions are seen in parts of Northern China where the predominance of wheat in the form of noodles and breads is apparent. Also in many important occasions the absence of rice is strange but true.

Forks and knives are considered inappropriate while eating traditional Chinese food. Chopsticks are primarily used to eat all kinds of food other than soups and other liquids which, are consumed with large spoons. Such importance is given to the use of chopsticks that in the bygone era, they were made of expensive materials like ivory and gold.
The Chinese believe in the concept of wholeness of being. For this purpose, fish, which is a very popular non-vegetarian item, is many times served whole. Chicken which is also very popular is cut into pieces. However, all its parts including the head and gizzards are served so that the wholeness of food remains intact. Contrary to popular belief, many Chinese are vegetarians and Tofu is not the only vegetable that is eaten at large. Other commonly eaten vegetables include pok choy, shiitake mushroom, sprouts and corn. These vegetables are given the texture of meat by using large amounts of soy and are called 'imitated meat'.

The Chinese do not round up their meals with dessert though some of their sweet preparations are a great favourite in many restaurants. Also no cold drinks are served during a meal because they are considered harmful when combined with hot food. Instead tea is served because it helps digestion.

Although, Chinese cuisine has its rules and regulations, it has evolved over the ages to adapt itself to alien conditions. For example, the Chinese tradition of using individual chopsticks to carve bite-sized portions of food from serving plates is scarcely practiced outside the country. Instead serving spoons are given to diners. Moreover, in many restaurants in the West, Chinese food is served with chilled beer because inhabitants there are acclimatized to such eating habits.

Chinese cuisine has universal appeal because it is not complicated in nature. Also modifications can be done to it according to one's palate and the food tastes as great as ever!

Veg Noodles Soup

Ingredients:

Water	: 2 cup	Cauliflower	: 6-8
Diced onion	: 1	Mushroom	: 8-10
Diced carrot	: 2	Light soya sauce	: 1 tsp
Chopped celery	: 1 tbsp	Salt	: to taste
Chopped leeks	: 2 tbsp	White pepper powder	: ½ tsp
Bayleaf	: 1	Sugar	: a pinch
Black pepper	: 6-8	Cornflower slurry	: 2 tsp
Cable leaves	: 5-6	Boiled noodels	: 3 tbsp
Baby corn	: 3-4	Chopped spring onion	: 3 tsp
Pokchoy	: 3-4	Chopped garlic	: 2 tsp

Procedure:

1) To begin preparing the vegetable stock by boiling water in a pan.
2) Add the chopped onion, carrot, chopped leeks & celery.
3) Now add bayleaf & black pepper, bring to a boil and for an hour.
4) Put in the blanched carrot and chinese cabbage along with baby corn, pok choy, cauliflower, mushroom and light soya sauce.
5) Now add salt, white pepper powder and sugar, add the cornflour paste for thickening of the soup. Stir and take off the heat after a boil.
6) Garnish with chopped spring onions and chopped fried garlic.

To serve: Place boiled noodles in a serving bowl and pour the soup over it.

Sizzling Rice Soup

A restaurant specialty, sizzling rice soup makes crackling sounds when crisp rice is added to the hot broth.

Serves: 6

Ingredients:

For sizzling rice Soup

Large dried black mushrooms, stems removed	: 4
Medium (about 6 ounces) boneless, skinless chicken breast	: 1
Sliced ginger	: 1
Barbequed pork (or cooked ham)	: ¼ cup
Shrimp	: 125 gms
Canned bamboo shoots	: ¼ cup
Canned water chestnuts	: ¼ cup
Chicken stock or broth	: 5 cups
Reserved mushroom soaking liquid	: 1 cup
Dark soy sauce	: 1 tbsp
Chinese rice wine or dry sherry	: 1½ tsp
Salt and pepper	: to taste
Sesame oil	: a few drops
Vegetable oil for deep-frying	

For baked sizzling rice

Long grain rice	: 1 cup
Water	: 1½ cups

Procedure:

1) In a pan of hot water, soak mushrooms for 20 minutes. Strain the liquid and reserve 1 cup for the soup.

2) Cut mushrooms into quarters and the water chestnuts and bamboo shoots into thin slices.

3) Put chicken and sliced ginger in a pot of boiling water and briefly blanch the chicken, until it changes colour.

4) Drain and cut the chicken into thin slices.

5) Bring the chicken stock or broth and the reserved mushroom liquid to a boil. Add the chicken and pork, shrimp and the vegetables. Let simmer for a few minutes.

6) Add the soy sauce, sherry, and the salt and pepper and drizzle with sesame oil.
7) Bring back to a boil and then let simmer for a few more minutes. Place the soup in a large serving bowl and keep warm.
8) Heat wok and add oil for deep-frying. When oil is ready, add the Crispy Rice. Deep-fry until it puffs and turns brown, then drain on paper towels.
9) Add the rice to the soup at the table, so that guests can hear the rice make popping sounds when added to the broth.

Procedure for baked sizzling rice

1) Rinse 1 cup of long or medium grain rice.
2) In a pot, add 1½ cups water (1¼ if using medium grain rice) to the rice and bring to a boil.
3) Cover and simmer on low heat for 30 minutes. Remove from burner and allow to cool.
4) While rice is cooling, preheat oven to 300° F.
5) Place the rice on a baking sheet, making sure that it is about, but no more than, ¼ inch thick.
6) Bake the rice for 50 - 55 minutes, until it is dry.
7) Cool and cut into 2" squares.
8) Store in a canister until needed. Do not freeze.
9) When serving, heat the soup and deep fry the squares and add to soup.

Hot & Sour Soup

Serves: 4

Ingredients:

Sliced mushrooms	: 3 tbsp	Green chilies, slit	: 3
Baby corns,		Seasoning vegetable cube	: 1
cut diagonally	: 7	Lemon juice	: 1 tsp
Cloves garlic	: 7		
Ginger, cut into thin		**For the garnish:**	
strips	: 50 mm	Spring onion, finely cut	: 2 tbsp
	(2") piece	Chopped coriander	: 2 tbsp
Lemon grass, tied	: 5 stalks	Carrots, cut into thin	
Chopped coriander	: ¼ cup	strips	: 2 tbsp

Procedure:

1) Using the strip of lemon grass, tie the lemon grass stalks and coriander together.
2) In a pan boil 5 cups of water and add the seasoning cube, garlic, ginger, lemon grass and coriander (tied together).
3) Cover and simmer for 15 minutes.
4) When the aroma starts getting released, the garlic, ginger, lemon grass and coriander bunch from the water.
5) Add the chilies, mushrooms, baby corn, salt and simmer for another 15 minutes in the covered pan. Add the lemon juice just before serving.
6) Garnish the soup bowl with spring onions, coriander and carrot, pour the hot soup over it and serve at once.

Tips:

* Since seasoning cubes already contain salt, take care to add extra salt last, if required. Pouring hot soup over the spring onions, carrots and coriander helps release their flavours besides cooking them slightly.

Chicken and Spinach Soup

Chicken and spinach soup - A very nutritious chicken soup made with fresh spinach leaves.

Serves: 4–6

Ingredients:

Skinless, boneless, chicken breast	: 170 gms	4 cups chicken stock, or 4 cups store-bought chicken broth mixed with 1 cup water	
Chinese rice wine or dry sherry	: 1 tbsp	Sliced ginger	: 1 tbsp
Sugar	: ¾ tsp	Soy sauce	: 1 tbsp
Sesame oil	: 1 tsp	Salt and pepper	: to taste
Fresh spinach leaves	: 250 gms		

Procedure:

1) Wash the chicken breast, pat dry, and cut into thin strips approximately 2 inches long and ⅛ inch thick.

2) In a medium bowl, add the rice wine, ½ tsp sugar and a few drops of sesame oil to chicken pieces and marinate the chicken for 20 minutes.

3) Meanwhile the spinach leaves and cut off the stems. Blanch the leaves in a large pot of boiling water for 1-2 minutes, or until the leaves turn a bright green.

4) Plunge the blanched leaves briefly in cold water first to stop the cooking process, and then drain thoroughly.

5) Bring the chicken stock or chicken broth and water to a boil. Stir in the soy sauce and remaining ¼ tsp sugar.

6) Add the chicken strips. Bring back to a boil and cook until the chicken turns white and is cooked through.

7) Add the ginger and spinach leaves and bring back to a boil. Stir in the soy sauce. Taste and adjust the seasoning if desired. Serve hot.

Sweet Corn Chicken Soup

Serves: 4

Ingredients:

Cooked chopped (or shredded) chicken	: 1 cup	Chopped spring onion	: ¼ cup
Cooked sweet corn kernels	: 1 cup	Corn flour	: 1 tbsp
Chicken stock	: 4 cups	Pepper as per taste	
Egg white, lightly beaten	: 1		

Procedure:

1) Boil the chicken stock in a vessel.
2) Add chicken pieces and corn kernels and continue to cook.
3) Meanwhile, dissolve corn flour in ¼ cup water.
4) Pour it into the stock and chicken being cooked taking care to stir continuously so no lump is formed.
5) Simmer the mix for ten minutes.
6) Now add spring onion and pepper and simmer for another 5-7 mins.
7) Slowly pour in egg white, stirring continuously.
8) Take off from fire immediately after putting the egg white.
9) Garnish with coriander leaves / chicken pieces / corn kernels.
10) Serve hot.

Chicken Wonton Soup

Serves: 4

Ingredients:

Ground chicken	: 200 gms	Hoisin sauce	: 1 tbsp
Cornstarch	: 2 tsp	Chopped green onions	: ¼ tsp
Refrigerated egg		Rice-wine vinegar	: 1 tbsp
substitute	: 2 tbsp	Egg roll wrappers	: 8
Ground ginger	: ¼ tsp	Granulated sugar	: 1 tbsp
Soy sauce; divided	: 3 tbsp	Chicken broth	: 4 cups
Black pepper	: ¼ tsp		

Procedure:

1) Mix the chicken and egg substitute in a bowl.
2) Add the soy sauce, hoisin sauce, vinegar, sugar, cornstarch, ginger, and pepper.
3) Stir in the green onions. Cover bowl with plastic wrap refrigerate for 15 minutes.
4) Place the chicken mixture evenly into center of each roll wrapper. Brush corners with water; press together to seal.
5) In a large pot, bring 2 litres of water to a boil over high heat. Add wontons.
6) Cook, stirring, until wontons float to surface, this takes about 10 minutes.
7) Meanwhile, in a medium saucepan, bring broth to a boil over medium heat.
8) Add remaining soy sauce.
9) Divide wontons evenly among individual serving bowls.
10) Pour soup over wontons and serve.

Tofu Sizzler

Serves: 2

Ingredients:

Olive oil	: 3-4 tsp	Black pepper	: to taste
Chopped red, green and		Mashed potato	: 1 cup
Yellow bell pepper	: 2-3 tbsp	Tofu pieces	: 6-7
Blanched beans	: 1-2 tbsp	Cabbage leaves	: 4-5
Chopped carrot	: 1 tbsp	Lettuce leaves	: 1-2
Blanched broccoli	: 4-5	Potato fingers	: 6-7
	florets	Butter	: 2-3 tsp
Salt	: to taste	Lemon juice	: 2-3 tsp

Procedure:

1) Heat olive oil in a pan and bell peppers, beans, carrot and broccoli.

2) Now add salt and pepper and toss.

3) Add some salt and pepper to the potatoes and mix well.

4) Coat the tofu pieces with potato mixture and fry.

5) Place cabbage and lettuce leaves on a sizzler plate.

6) Place the tofu stuffed potato cake and potato fingers.

7) Add butter and lemon juice.

8) Tofu sizzler is ready to serve.

Cottage Cheese & Spinach Wonton

Serves: 2–3

Ingredients:

Oil	: 2½ cup	Salt	: to taste
Chopped garlic	: 1 tsp	White pepper powder	: 1 tsp
Cottage cheese	: ⅓ cup	Wonton skin	: 8-10 nos.
Shredded spinach	: ½ cup	Water	: ½ cup

Procedure:

1) Heat oil in a wok and also heat a little oil in a pan for sauteing the stuffing.
2) First fry chopped garlic and onion in the pan. When brown add crumbled cottage cheese and cook till dry.
3) Add shredded spinach and or salt and white pepper powder and mix well.
4) Place it in a bowl and let it cool.
5) Once stuffing has cooled, stuff wonton skin with this and seal with water from all 4 sides.
6) Now deep fry wontons till light brown and place them in a serving dish to serve hot.

Note:

• Cottage cheese leaves water during cooking, so make sure to dry it out thoroughly.

Chicken Spring Rolls

Ingredients:

Vegetable oil	: 2 tbsp	Hoisin sauce	: 1 tbsp
Minced garlic	: 1 tbsp	Oyster sauce	: 1 tbsp
Grated ginger	: ½ tbsp	Chopped coriander	: 2 tbsp
Shredded Napa cabbage	: 2 cups	Package spring roll	
Carrot, grated	: 1	wrappers	: 1
Bean sprouts	: ½ cup	Egg, beaten	: 1
Bean thread noodles,		Vegetable oil	: for frying
blanched and chopped	: 60 gms		
Shredded cooked			
chicken breast	: 250 gms		

Procedure:

1) Cook the garlic, ginger, cabbage, carrot, and bean sprouts in a wok for 2 minutes.

2) Add the noodles and chicken; continue to cook until heated through.

3) Pour the hoisin and oyster sauces, toss to coat the mixture. The filling should be moist but not wet.

4) Remove from heat, and allow to cool. Then toss in the chopped coriander.

5) Lay a spring roll wrapper on a flat surface on an angle so it looks like a diamond. Put 2 tablespoons of the filling near the bottom corner of the wrapper and fold up to enclose the filling. Fold in the 2 sides. Paint the top seam of the wrapper with beaten egg. Continue rolling up to form a tight cylinder.

6) Pour about 1-inch of oil in a skillet and heat to 350° F. Fry the spring rolls for 2 minutes, turning to cook all sides. Drain on paper towels before serving.

Vegetable Siew Mai

Serves: 2

Ingredients:

Wonton skin	: 8 pcs	Cottage cheese	: 50 gms
Cabbage, juliennes	: 100 gms	Salt	: 1 tsp
Carrot, juliennes	: 100 gms	Red chilli powder	: ¼ tsp
Broccoli florets	: 100 gms	White pepper powder	: ¼ tsp
Boiled potatoes	: 50 gms	Sesame oil	: 1 tsp

Procedure:

1) Blanch all the vegetables in salted boiling water.
2) Drain and pour cold water to cool the vegetables.
3) Squeeze a bit and finally drop all the vegetables.
4) Squeeze again to remove all moisture in a muslin cloth.
5) Add 50 gms of finely grated boiled potatoes and 50 gms of finely grated cottage cheese.
6) Now add salt, red chilli powder, white pepper and sesame oil and mix things up well.
7) Cut the wonton skin in round shape.
8) Put 1-½ tsp of mixture and press down to form the dim sum.
9) Repeat it for the entire mixture.
10) In a steaming basket put a banana leaf slightly greased with oil.
11) Place dim sum in the basket; cover with lid and steam for 3-4 minutes or till the wonton skin is cooked.
12) Serve hot with soya sesame dip.

Chinese Sweet and Sour Chicken Legs

Ingredients:

Chicken Legs	: 6	Big onion finely chopped	: 1
Tomato sauce	: 4 tbsp	Dry red chilli deseed &	
Vinegar	: 2 tbsp	tear into pieces	
Soya sauce	: ½ tsp	(or chopped green chillis)	: 2
Red chilli powder	: ½ tsp	Grated ginger-garlic	
Black pepper powder	: ¼ tsp	(optional)	: 1 tsp
Salt	: to taste	Oil	: 1 tbsp

Procedure:

1) Wash chicken and drain water completely. Marinate the chicken with tomato sauce, vinegar, soya sauce, red chilli powder and pepper powder for half an hour.

2) Heat a vessel and add the marinated chicken and let the chicken cook in its own juices there is no need to add water.

3) Cover and cook till the chicken absorbs all the spices and sauces. Keep checking and stirring so that it doesn't burn.

4) Meanwhile heat oil in a pan and add the onions, chillis and garlic-ginger and fry well on high heat stirring continuosly till well browned. Add the fried chicken legs and stir fry for 4-5 minutes till well roasted and coated with the onions. Serve hot with salad.

Spiced Chinese Fish Fillet

Serves: 3

Ingredients:

Fish fillets	: 6	Vinegar	: 1 tbsp
Chinese 5 spices powder		Ginger garlic paste	: 1 tbsp
(equal parts of cinnamon,		Salt	: to taste
fennel, star anise, cloves		Rice flour	: ¼ cup
and black pepper)	: 1 tsp	Oil for frying	
Soya sauce(optional)	: 1 tsp		

Procedure:

1) Mix all the above ingredients except rice flour and salt and marinate the fish fillets with this mixture and keep aside for ½ hr.

2) Dust the marinated fish fillets with the rice flour and salt.

3) Heat 1-2 tbsp oil in a frying pan to medium-high and fry 2 fish fillets at a time for 2-4 minutes each side till golden brown. Pat dry with paper towel when done. Serve hot with salad.

Note:

• Alternately, you can also dip the marinated fish fillets in all purpose flour, then dip in beaten eggs and then coat in bread crumbs before shallow frying.

Crab Rangoon

Ingredients:

Cream cheese	: 250 gms	Large clove garlic,	
Fresh crab meat or		smashed, peeled, and	
canned crab meat,		finely minced	: 1
drainedand flaked	: 250 gms	Package wonton	
Red onion, chopped	: 1 tsp	wrappers	: 1
Worcestershire sauce	: ½ tsp	Small bowl water	: 1
Light soy sauce	: ½ tsp	Oil for deep-frying	
Freshly ground			
black pepper	: to taste		
Green onion, finely sliced	: 1		

Procedure:

1) Take the cream cheese and crab meat and combine well in a bowl. Add the remaining six filling ingredients (up to the wonton wrappers) one at a time, mixing as you go from one to the next.

2) On a flat surface, lay out a wonton wrapper in front of you so that it forms 2 triangles (not a square). Wet the edges of the won ton.

3) Add 1 tsp of filling to the middle, and spread it out toward the left and right points of the wrapper so that it forms a log or rectangular shape (otherwise the wrapper may break in the middle during deep-frying).

4) Fold over the edges of the wrapper to make a triangle. Wet the edges with water and press together to seal.

5) Cover the made Crab Rangoon with a damp cloth or paper towel to keep them from drying out while preparing the rest.

6)   Heat wok and add oil for deep-frying. When oil is ready (the temperature should be between 360° - 375°), carefully slide in the Crab Rangoon, taking care not to overcrowd the wok. Deep-fry until they are golden brown, about 3 minutes, turning once. Remove with a slotted spoon and drain.

7)   Serve hot with Sweet and Sour Sauce or Chinese Hot Mustard.

Note:
- Never overcrowd the wok. Give the wontons space to fry evenly.

Crispy Honey Chicken

Serves: 4

Ingredients:

Boneless, skinless chicken
breast, cut into medium
size chunks : 450 gms
Minced garlic : 1 tbsp
Vegetable oil : for frying
Red bell pepper and/or scallions,
julliene
Crispy noodles, rice or egg noodles or
steamed rice for serving

Batter:
All purpose flour : 120 gms
Cornstarch : 75 gms
Egg : 1
Water : 90 ml
Baking powder : ⅛ tsp
Baking soda : ⅛ tsp

Chicken Seasoning:
Lite soy sauce : 1 tbsp
White pepper : ⅛ tsp
Kosher salt : ¼ tsp
Corn starch : 1 tbsp

Sauce:
Sake or rice wine : ½ cup
Honey : ½ cup
Rice vinegar : 90 ml
Lite soy sauce : 3 tbsp
Sugar : 6 tbsp
Cornstarch slurry : ¼ cup corn
starch mixed with ¼ cup water

Procedure:

1) Mix together all the batter ingredients and place in refrigerator for 2 hrs.

2) Coat chicken well with seasonings and marinate in the refrigerator for 20 minutes.

3) In a large bowl mix the sauce ingredients thoroughly and reserve.

4) Pour vegetable oil into a heavy bottomed wok and slowly heat to 340°-350°.

5) Put ¼ of the marinated chicken in a clean bowl and pour enough batter over to coat.

6) *Remove a few pieces at a time from the batter, using slotted spoon or large fork. Shake off excess batter. Carefully lower chicken into the hot oil.*

7) *Fry the chicken until the batter "sets," 20-30 seconds and it becomes golden and crisp.*

8) *Remove to platter with paper towels to drain. Repeat for all the chicken.*

9) *Now bring the reserved sauce to a boil in a saucepan.*

10) *Add cornstarch slurry, a little at a time. The sauce will thicken, as it cooks for a minute or two.*

11) *In a wok add 2 tbsp oil and heat.*

12) *Put in the minced garlic, red bell pepper and scallions and stir-fry briefly.*

13) *Add ⅓ to ½ of the chicken (depending on pan size) and stir-fry briefly. Add enough sauce to just coat chicken.*

14) *Fry for a little longer and then spoon hot over rice to serve.*

Hot and Sour Chinese Eggplant

Serves: 2

Ingredients:

Long Chinese eggplants, cubed	: 2	Cornstarch	: 1 tsp
Soy sauce	: 1½ tbsp	Chili oil	: ½ tsp
Red wine vinegar	: 1 tbsp	Salt	: 2 tsp
White sugar	: 1 tbsp	Vegetable oil	: 2 tbsp
Green chili pepper, chopped	: 1		

Procedure:

1) Place the eggplant cubes into a large bowl, and sprinkle with salt. Fill with enough water to cover, and let stand for 30 minutes.

2) Rinse well, and drain on paper towels.

3) In a small bowl, stir together the soy sauce, red wine vinegar, sugar, chile pepper, cornstarch and chili oil.

4) Set the sauce aside.

5) Heat the vegetable oil in a large skillet or wok over medium-high heat.

6) Fry the eggplant until it is tender and begins to brown, 5 to 10 minutes.

7) Pour in the sauce, and cook and stir until the sauce is thick and the eggplant is evenly coated.

8) Serve immediately.

Assorted Mushroom with Oyster Sauce

Serves: 4

Ingredients:

Large Shitake Mushroom, sliced thick	: 6	White Button Mushroom, sliced thick	: 1 pack
Shimeiji Mushroom, end, chopped	: 1 pack	Oyster sauce	: 1½ tbsp
		Oil	: 1 tbsp

Procedure:

1) Heat oil in wok.

2) Saute the mushroom till it's slightly brown.

3) Remove into a dish and keep aside.

4) Using the same wok (do not clean away the oil), add in the oyster sauce.

5) When the oyster sauce starts to cook and thicken, add the mushroom and coat well.

6) serve on a bed of rice.

Note:

• If you prefer you can also make vegetables in oyster sauce.

Green Beans in Black Bean Sauce

Ingredients:

Fresh green beans	: 500 gms	Cold water	: ¼ cup
Black bean paste	: 2 tbsp	Corn starch	: 1 tbsp
Low sodium soy sauce	: 2 tbsp		

Procedure:

1) Wash green beans and trim into bite sized pieces. Steam or microwave with a little water until just tender. Drain and rinse with cold water to stop cooking.

2) Mix together the black bean paste, soy sauce, water and corn starch until very smooth.

3) Heat a wok or large saucepan to medium high. Add some water and the cooked beans. When beans are heated (about 2 minutes) add the sauce. Stir constantly to coat the beans (sauce will get very thick). Serve immediately over hot cooked rice.

Walnuts in Sweet and Sour Sauce

Serves: 4

Ingredients:

Materials:			
Walnuts	: 150 gms	Salt	: ½ tbsp
Canned Pineapple	: 2 slices	Water	: 100 ml
Green Pepper	: 1 pc		
Red Pepper	: 2 pc	**Sauce:**	
		Corn Flour	: 2 tbsp
Seasoning:		Water	: 7 tbsp
Plain Flour	: 150 ml	White Vinegar	: 2 tbsp
Corn Flour	: 1 tbsp	Sugar	: 4 tbsp
Baking Powder	: 1 tbsp	Tomato Ketchup	: 3 tbsp

Procedure:

1) Mix seasoning well, then add 1 tbsp of oil and mix well again.

2) Mix sauce well, for further use.

3) Remove membrane of walnuts, parboil in hot water for 1 minute, drain.

4) Heat 500 ml of water, boil walnut 3-5 minutes with 1 tbsp of salt until soft.

5) Marinate boiled walnuts into mixed seasoning, coat each walnuts with batter.

6) Heat wok with oil, deep fry the coated walnuts until crispy, drain dry.

7) Chop red and green pepper, pineapple into small cubes.

8) Heat wok with 2 tbsp of oil, stir fry chopped pepper and pineapple.

9) Add in mixed sauce, stir fry until boiling.

10) Add in the walnuts and serve.

Vegetables in Spicy Almond Sauce

Serves: 4

Ingredients:

Vegetables (baby corn, broccoli, carrots), cut into wedges (parboiled)	: 2 cups	**Ingredients for Chinese white sauce:**	
Fresh red chillies, sliced	: 1 tsp	Onions (finely chopped)	: ½ cup
Almonds (blanched, peeled and sliced)	: ½ cup	Ginger (chopped)	: 2 tsp
		Garlic (chopped)	: 2 tsp
Bean sprouts	: ¼ cup	White wine	: ½ cup
Chinese white sauce	: 2 cups	Cornflour	
Oil	: 1 tbsp	(mixed with 3 cups of clear vegetable stock)	: 2 tbsp
Salt	: to taste		
		Sugar	: a pinch
		Oil	: 1 tbsp
		Salt	: to taste

Procedure:

1) Heat the oil, add the fresh red chillies, almonds, bean sprouts and vegetables and sauté for a few seconds.
2) Add the Chinese white sauce and salt and bring to a boil.
3) Serve immediately.

Procedure for Chinese white sauce:

1) Heat the oil in a pan, add the onions, ginger and garlic and sauté till the onions are translucent.

2) *Add the wine and cook on a high flame for a few seconds.*

3) *Add the cornflour paste and cook till the sauce thickens.*

4) *Add sugar and salt, mix well and use as required.*

Notes:

- *To blanch the almonds, boil water and take off the flame. Add almonds to the hot water and keep aside for 10 to 15 minutes.*
- *The skin will loosen thus making it easy to peel the almonds.*

Almond Chicken

Serves: 4

Ingredients:

Skinned chicken breast	: 500 gms	Green pepper, chopped as above	: 1
Vegetable oil	: 1 cup	Diced bamboo shoots	: ½ cup
Fresh ginger root	: 5 slices	Slivered almonds	: ⅓
Green onions, chopped to about 1" lengths	: 3		

Procedure:

1) Dice chicken into 1 inch cubes.

2) Combine marinade ingredients, add chicken and mix well.

3) Let stand for ½ hour. Heat oil in a wok, add chicken and stir fry until browned. Remove chicken and drain well.

4) Stir fry ginger, onion, pepper and bamboo shoots for about 1 minute until vegetables are crisp-tender. Combine ingredients for seasoning sauce in a small bowl, mix well and add to wok. Bring to boil.

5) Add chicken to boiling sauce. Stir fry chicken until coated with sauce. Add almonds, mix well and serve hot.

Diced Chicken in Hot Garlic Sauce

Serves: 4

Ingredients:

Chicken breasts and thighs	: 200g	Stock	: 1 cup
Cornstarch	: 2 tsp dissovled in 2 tbsp water	Sesame oil	: 1 tsp
		Water chestnuts	: 5
		Hot red chili pepper	: 1
		Vegetable oil	: ½ cup (100ml)
Salt	: ⅛ tsp or to taste	Ginger slices	: 1 tsp
		Scallions, chopped	: 2 tsp
Rice wine	: 2 tsp	Garlic slices	: 1 tsp
Soy sauce	: 1.5 tsp	Rice vinegar	: ⅛ tsp

Procedure:

1) Dice the chicken into even 1" cubes.
2) Mix together 1 tbsp of the cornstarch-water mixture with the salt and 1 tsp of the rice wine.
3) Coat the chicken well with this mixture and set aside.
4) Now take another bowl and in it mix the soy sauce, the remaining 1 tsp rice wine, the stock, the other 1 tbsp of cornstarch, and the sesame oil to the consistency of a sauce and set aside.
5) Peel and dice the water chestnuts. Seed the chili pepper and chop finely.
6) Heat the oil in a wok and add the chicken and chili pepper, stir fry until the chicken turns red.
7) Add the ginger, water chestnuts, scallions and garlic, and fry until fragrant.
8) Stir in the sauce and sprinkle with the vinegar. Stir fry for a minute and serve.

Chicken Manchurian

Serves: 4

Ingredients:

Chicken (cut into 1 inch squares)	: ½ kg	Green Chili (crushed)	: 2 tbsp
Corn Flour	: ½ tbsp	Cilantro (chopped)	: 2 tbsp
Egg (beaten)	: 1	Chicken Stock	: 1 cup
All Purpose Flour	: ½ tbsp	Soya Sauce	: 1 tbsp
Salt	: to taste	Salt	: ¼ tsp
Ground Black Pepper	: to taste	Ground Black Pepper	: ¼ tsp
Cooking Oil	: 2 tbsp	Sugar	: ¼ tsp
Ginger (crushed)	: 2 tbsp	Corn Flour (extra)	
Garlic (crushed)	: 2 tbsp	dissolved in ¼ cup water	: 2 tbsp

Procedure:

1) First mix corn flour, flour, salt and pepper with the beaten egg to make the batter.

2) Now dip the chicken pieces in the batter, deep fry till golden brown. Keep aside.

3) For the sauce, heat oil in a pan. Lightly fry garlic and ginger till they just change colour.

4) Now add green chilies and cilantro leaves. Fry for a minute.

5) Then reduce the heat, add chicken stock, soya sauce, salt, sugar, pepper. Cook for another 5 minutes.

6) Add corn flour mixed with water and give one boil.

7) Finally add the fried chicken Manchurian to the sauce and cook for 1-2 minutes. Serve hot.

Ginger Chicken

Ingredients:

Boneless, skinless chicken		Water	: ½ cup
breasts	: 4	Soy sauce	: 2 tbsp
Oil, divided	: 1 tbsp	Seasoned rice vinegar	: 2 tbsp
Medium red bell pepper,		Grated, peeled ginger root	: 1 tbsp
thinly sliced	: 1	Chopped green onions	: garnish

Procedure:

1) In a wok heat half the oil and saute chicken breasts until cooked.

2) Remove the chicken from the pan.

3) Now heat the remaining oil and add the bell peppers cooking until tender.

4) Stir in water, soy sauce, vinegar, gingerroot and let boil for a minute.

5) Return chicken to pan; sprinkle with onions and serve.

Duck with Mushrooms

Serves: 4–6

Ingredients:

Ducks, cut in pieces	: 2	Butter	: 3 tbsp
Clove garlic, minced	: 1	Small jar pearl onions	
Thyme	: ⅛ tsp	(about 12)	: 1
Ham, in ¼" cubes	: 100 gms	Flour	: 1 tbsp
Fresh parsley, chopped	: 1 tsp	Salt and pepper	: to taste
Mushrooms, sliced thick	: 250 gms		

Procedure:

1) Brown the pieces of duck in the butter. When browned, add the ham, mushrooms, garlic, thyme, and flour. Saute for 10 minutes, stirring often.

2) Add enough water to cover the mixture half-way. Simmer for 15 minutes. Add onions, and the salt & pepper, to taste, and simmer for another 15 minutes, or until done.

Sweet and Sour Chicken

Ingredients:

Pineapple chunks, drained	: 200 gms	Self-rising flour	: 2¼ cups
Green bell pepper, cut into 1 inch pieces	: 2	Vegetable oil	: 2 tbsp
		Cornstarch	: 2 tbsp
Cornstarch	: ¼ cup	Salt	: ½ tsp
Water	: 1¾ cups	Ground white	: ¼ tsp
White sugar	: ¾ cup	Pepper	:
Distilled white vinegar	: ½ cup	Egg	: 1
Orange food color	: 2 drops	Water	: 2 cups
Skinless, boneless chicken breast halves - cut into 1 inch cubes	: 8	Vegetable oil for frying	: 1 quart

Procedure:

1) Put 1½ cups water, sugar, vinegar, reserved pineapple syrup, and orange food coloring in a saucepan and bring to a boil.

2) Take the pan off the heat. Mix the cornstarch with ¼ cup water and slowly stir into saucepan. Continue stirring until mixture thickens.

3) Combine flour, 2 tablespoons oil, 2 tablespoons cornstarch, salt, white pepper, and egg. Add 1½ cups water gradually to make a thick batter. Stir to blend thoroughly.

4) Add chicken pieces, and stir until chicken is well coated.

5) Heat oil in skillet or wok to 360° F (180° C). Fry chicken pieces in hot oil until golden. Remove chicken, and drain on paper towels.

6) When ready to serve, layer green peppers, pineapple chunks, and cooked chicken pieces on a platter. Pour hot sweet and sour sauce over top.

Fish with Black Bean Sauce

Serves: 4

Ingredients:

Fresh fish, boned, cut into fillets	: 450 gms	Soy sauce	: 2 tbsps
Rice wine	: 1 tbsp	Corn starch	: 1 tbsp
Salt	: ½ tsp	Fermented black beans, minced	: 2 tbsps
Sesame oil	: 1 tbsp	Garlic, minced	: 2 cloves
Oil	: 1 tbsp	Green onions, sliced	: 4
Sugar	: 1 tsp		

Procedure:

1) Cut fish into 2-inch pieces.

2) Mix rice wine and salt together in a large bowl and add the fish pieces. Coat well and let sit for 15 minutes.

3) Remove from marinade and pat dry.

4) To the reserved marinade, add the oils, sugar, soy sauce, cornstarch, black beans, and garlic. Mix well.

5) Pour water into a wok about ⅔ full. Heat the water to boiling.

6) Dip fish pieces in the sauce and place on a rack that sits over the wok.

7) Cover and steam fish for about 20 minutes. Fish should be white and firm to the touch.

8) Serve immediately, sprinkled with green onions.

Spicy Shredded Lamb

Ingredients:

Lean boneless lamb	: 400 gms	Vegetable oil	: 2 tbsp
Large onion (sliced)	: 1	Toasted sesame	
Garlic (chopped fine)	: 1 tsp	seeds (optional)	: 2 tsp
Fresh ginger (grated)	: 2 tsp	Sliced spring onions or	
Dark soya sauce	: 1 tbsp	cilantro leaves	: to garnish
Dry sherry	: 1 tbsp	Red and green chillies	: to garnish
Cornflour	: 2 tsp		
Sesame oil	: 1 tbsp		

Procedure:

1) Shred the lamb finely.

2) In a bowl, combine the garlic, ginger, soy sauce, sherry, sesame oil and cornflour.

3) Mix well then add lamb.

4) Marinate for at least 2 hours.

5) Heat oil in wok.

6) Stir-fry slices of onion briefly.

7) Remove and stir-fry the meat for about 1 to 2 minutes or till just about cooked.

8) Return onions to wok and stir-fry for another 1 minute or so.

9) Remove and place on a serving dish.

10) Sprinkle with toasted sesame seeds and garnish with spring onions or cilantro leaves, and the two kinds of chillies.

Prawns with Hot Bean Sauce

Serves: 12

Ingredients:

Prawns peeled and deveined	: 500 gms	Chicken broth or water	: 1 tbsp

Marinade:

Other:

Egg white	: 1	Cornstarch	: 1 tsp
Salt	: 1 tsp	Water	: 2 tbsp
Cornstarch,	: 1 tbsp or	Green onion, chopped	: ½
	: as needed	Ginger, finely chopped	: 1 tbsp
		Oil for deep-frying	: 4 cups
		Salt	: ½ tsp or to taste

Sauce:

Ketchup	: 4 tbsp	Sugar	: ½ tsp or to taste
Hot bean sauce	: 1 tbsp		
Chinese rice wine or dry sherry	: 1 tbsp	Lettuce leaves, shredded	: 3 to 4
		Lemons, cut into wedges	: 2

Procedure:

1) Rinse the prawns under warm running water and pat dry. Leave whole, or cut in half lengthwise if desired.

2) Use your fingers to mix in the marinade ingredients. Marinate the prawns for 30 minutes.

3) In a small bowl, mix together the sauce ingredients. Set aside.

4) In another small bowl, dissolve the cornstarch in 2 tablespoons water. Set aside. Chop the green onion and ginger.

5) Heat the oil in a wok to about 300° F. When the oil is hot, add the marinated prawns.

Deep-fry until they change colour and are nearly cooked. Remove from the wok with a slotted spoon and drain.

6) *Leave all but 2 tablespoons oil in the wok and remove the rest.*

7) *Add the ginger and green onion and stir-fry until aromatic. Add the sauce ingredients.*

• *Give the cornstarch and water mixture a quick re-stir and add to the sauce, stirring quickly to thicken.*

8) *Add the prawns back into the wok. Sprinkle the salt and sugar over top.*

9) *Serve the prawns on top of the torn lettuce leaves, with lemon wedges for garnish.*

Kung Pao Chicken

Ingredients:

Chicken, boneless & skinless	: 400 gms	Cornstarch	: 1 tsp
Cooking oil	: 2½ tbsp	Black vinegar or balsamic vinegar	: ¼ cup
Small dried red chilies	: 8	Chicken broth	: ¼ cup
Minced garlic	: 4 tsp	Rice wine or dry sherry	: 3 tbsp
Ribs celery, diced	: 2	Sesame oil	: 2 tsp
Red bell pepper, cut into 1" squares	: ½	Sugar	: 2 tsp
Diced bamboo shoots	: ½ cup		
Cornstarch	: 2 tsp in 1 tbsp water	**Sauce ingredients:**	
		Oyster flavoured sauce	: 2 tbsp
		Hoisin sauce	: 2 tbsp
toasted walnut halves	: ½ cup	Soy sauce	: 1 tbsp
		Chili garlic sauce	: 2 tsp

Marinade ingredients:

Procedure:

1) Cut chicken into 1" pieces. Combine marinade ingredients in a bowl. Add chicken and stir to coat. Let stand for 10 minutes. Combine sauce ingredients in a bowl and set aside.

2) Place a wok over high heat until hot. Add 2 tbsp of oil, swirling to coat sides. Add chilies and cook, stirring, until fragrant, for about 10 seconds.

3) Add chicken and stir fry for 2 minutes. Remove the chicken and chilies from the wok.

4) *Add remaining ½ tbsp of oil, swirling to coat sides. Add garlic and cook, stirring, until fragrant, for about 10 seconds.*
5) *Add celery, bell pepper, and bamboo shoots; stir-fry for 1½ minutes. Return chicken and chilies to wok; stir-fry for 1 minute. Add sauce and bring to a boil.*
6) *Add cornstarch solution and cook, stirring, until sauce boils and thickens. Add walnuts and toss to coat.*

Pineapple Fried Rice

Serves: 2–3

Ingredients:

Cooked plain leftover rice	: 200 gms	Chopped pineapple	: 70-80 gms
Eggs	: 1		
Light soya	: 1 tbsp	Salt	: to taste
Raisins	: 30 gms	Pepper	: a pinch
Cashew nuts	: 30 gms	Oil	: 1 tbsp
Spring onions	: 40 gms		

Procedure:

1) Heat oil in a wok.

2) Put the beaten eggs.

3) Add the cooked plain rice and stir-fry.

4) Add rest of the ingredients.

5) Toss until everything is mixed.

6) Garnish with spring onion. Serve it in an emptied pineapple shell or plate.

Chicken Fried Rice

Chicken fried rice is a healthy, one dish meal. Like all fried rice dishes, Chicken fried rice tastes best when using leftover cooked rice.

Serves: 3

Ingredients:

Cold cooked rice	: 4 cups	**Seasonings (add according to taste):**	
Cooked chicken (chopped)	: 2 cups	Light Soy Sauce	
Eggs (more if desired)	: 2	Oyster sauce	
Green peas	: ½ cup	Salt	
Medium onion, diced	: 1	Pepper	
Green onion, diced	: 1	Oil for stir-frying, as needed	

Procedure:

1) Beat the eggs lightly with chopsticks, add a dash of salt (Add a bit of oyster sauce if desired).

2) Chop the chicken meat and dice the onion and green onion. Heat wok and add oil. When oil is ready, pour ½ of the egg mixture into the wok and cook over medium heat, turning over once. Cook the other half the same way. Cut the egg into thin strips, and save for later.

3) Stir-fry the onion on high heat for a few moments, remove and set aside. Do the same for the green peas.

4) Add oil, turn down the heat to medium and stir-fry the rice. Add the soy sauce, salt, pepper and oyster sauce. Add the chicken, onion and green peas and combine thoroughly. Serve chicken fried rice with the strips of egg on top and the green onion as a garnish.

Vegetable Noodles

Serves: 2

Ingredients:

Noodles (cooked)	: 250 gms	Spring onions	: ½ cup
Chinese all spice powder	: 2 tsps	Chilly powder	: 1 tsp
Frozen vegetables	: 1 cup		(optional)
Soya sauce	: 2 tsp	Water	: as needed
Tomato sauce	: 2 tsp	Oil	: 4 tsp
Onion (chopped)	: 1 cup		
Green chllies (finely chopped)	: 4		

Procedure:

1) Cook frozen vegetables by adding a dash of all spice powder for 10 minutes.

2) Heat oil in a wok.

3) Fry onion until it turns transparent.

4) Add green chillies and cooked vegetables and stir.

5) Meanwhile cook noodles as per pocket instructions or as required. Add cooked noodles into the fried onion and keep stiring for about 2 mins.

6) Add the balance all spice powder and mix into the noodle mixture.

7) Add soy sauce, tomato sauce and water and mix well.

8) Cover the wok and let the noodles cook for 5-8 mins.

9) Remove cover and stir for few more mins.

10) Remove from flame.

11) Garnish with spring onions and serve.

Crispy Noodles

Ingredients:

Raw rice noodles	: 60 gms	Vegetable stock	: ½ cup
Tofu or cottage cheese,		Chili powder	: ½ tsp
cut into strips	: 1 cup	Oil	: 2 tbsps
Oil for deep frying		Salt	: to taste

For the sauce		**For the garnish:**	
Garlic cloves, chopped	: 2	Red cabbage, diced	: ½ cup
Onion, sliced	: 1	Bean sprouts	: ⅓ cup
Soya sauce	: 1 tbsp	Spring onion, chopped	: 1
Sugar	: 4 tbsps	Cauliflower florets	: ½ cup
Lemon juice	: 1 ½ tbsp	Fresh red chili, slit	: 1

Procedure:

1) Heat the oil and deep fry the raw noodles till golden. Drain and keep aside.

2) Deep fry the tofu till crisp. Drain and keep aside.

3) For the sauce, heat the oil in a pan, add the garlic and onion and saute till brown.

4) Add the soya sauce, sugar, lemon juice, stock and salt and stir till the mixture begins to caramelise.

5) Add the fried tofu, chilli powder and mix well.

6) To proceed, Pour over the fried noodles, just before serving.

7) Serve garnished with the red cabbage, bean sprouts and spring onion and cauliflower and top with the red chili.

Hakka Noodles

Serves: 3–4

Ingredients:

Boiled flat noodles (marketed also as hakka noodles)	: 2 cups	Garlic finely chopped	: 2 tsp
		Vinegar	: ½ tsp
		Salt	: to taste
Dried red chilies	: 3	Oil	: 1½ tbsp
Small bunch spring onion	: 1	A pinch of Tandoori color	
Small capsicum thinly sliced	: 1		

Procedure:

1) Chop the spring onions into ¼″ pieces slanting. Pound red chilies and garlic coarsely.

2) Heat 1 tbsp oil in a wok, add chili and garlic and fry for a minute. Add the capsicum and fry till tender.

3) Add the spring onion and fry again for 2-3 minutes. Also add noodles and salt and mix well.

4) Now add tandoori color and vinegar to taste. Heat very well in oven or microwave before serving.

5) Serve with Schezwan sauce or Manchurian in gravy.

Mixed Meat Chow Mein

Ingredients:

Small shrimps (shelled or de-shelled)	: 125 gms	Soy sauce (for chicken)	: ½ tbsp
Chicken tenderloin	: 125 gms	Cornstarch (for chicken)	: 1 tsp
Pork tenderloin	: 125 gms	Soy sauce (for noodles)	: 1 tbsp
Black mushrooms	: 4 dried	Sesame oil (for noodles)	: 1 tbsp
Spinach	: 60 gms	Soy sauce	: 1 tbsp
Shredded green onion	: ⅓ cup	Salt	: 1 tsp
Dry noodle		Soup stock	: 2 cups
(thin or spaghetti)	: 450 gms	Cooking oil	: 10 tbsp
Shredded bamboo shoots	: ½ cup	Sesame oil	: ½ tbsp
Salt (for shrimp)	: ½ tsp		
Cornstarch (for shrimp)	: 1 tsp	**Cornstarch Paste:**	
Soy sauce (for pork)	: ½ tbsp	Cornstarch	: 2 tbsp
Cornstarch (for pork)	: 1 tsp	Water	: 2 tbsp

Procedure:

1) Soak the black mushrooms in hot water for an hour to soften them.

2) Then cut them into thin strips.

3) Shred the spinach into 1" long strips.

4) Clean the shrimps and mix them well with salt and cornstarch.

5) Cut the pork tenderloins into strings and mix well with soy sauce and cornstarch. Repeat the same step for the chicken tenderloins.

6) Boil the noodles in water for 3 minutes. Then rinse with cold water, and drain well.

7) Now put the noodles in a bowl, add the soy sauce and sesame oil and mix well.

8) Heat 4 tablespoons of cooking oil in a wok, pour all the noodles in. Fry for about 3 minutes until the bottom is brown. Turn them over, adding 2 more tablespoons of cooking oil around the edge of the pan.

9) Remove once both sides are browned.

10) Heat 4 tablespoons of cooking oil and stir fry the pork tenderloin strings first. When they turn white, remove them to a bowl.

11) Using the same cooking oil, stir fry the shrimps. When the shrimps turn pink, add the chicken tenderloins, then add the cornstarch paste.

12) Stir fry briefly, and then add the spinach, green onion and fried pork. Continue to stir fry, and then splash on the sesame oil, mix again and pour over prepared noodles.

13) Transfer everything on to a large plate, and serve.

Chinese Almond Cookies

Chinese almond cookies are a popular treat at Chinese bakeries.

Makes: *30 cookies*

Ingredients:

Flour	: 2 cups	Eggs	: 2
Baking powder	: ½ tsp	Almond extract	: 2½ tbsp
Baking soda	: ½ tsp	Whole, blanched	
Salt	: ⅛ tsp	almonds	: one for
Butter	: ½ cup		each cookie
Shortening	: ½ cup	Egg, lightly beaten	: 1
3/4 cup white sugar (can add up to 2 more tablespoons, if desired)			

Procedure:

1) Preheat oven to 325° F (162.5° C).

2) Sift the flour, baking powder, baking soda, and salt in a large bowl.

3) Take another bowl, and put the butter, shortening and sugar blending with a mixer.

4) Add eggs and almond extract and blend well. Add entire mix to the flour mix to form a crumbly mixture.

5) Use your fingers to form the mixture into a dough, and then form the dough into 2 rolls or logs that are 10 to 12 inches long. Wrap and refrigerate for 2 hours (this will make it easier to shape the dough into circles).

6) Take a log and lightly score the dough at 3/4 inch intervals so that you have 15 pieces and cut the dough. Roll each piece into a ball and place on a lightly greased cookie tray, approximately 1½ inches apart. Place an almond in the center of each cookie and press down lightly. Repeat with the remaining dough.

7) Brush each cookie lightly with beaten egg before baking. Bake for 15 minutes to 18 minutes, until golden brown. Cool and store in a sealed container.

Candied Banana Fritters

Serves: 4

Ingredients:

		Batter:	
Bananas	: 4	Egg	: 1
Cooking oil	: 1 tbsp	Cornstarch	: 4 tbsp
Sugar	: 6 tbsp	Flour	: 5 tbsp
Cold water	: 2 tbsp	Cold water	: 5 tbsp
Cooking oil	: 6 cups		
Sesame oil	: 2 tbsp		

Procedure:

1) *Beat the egg in a small bowl, add cornstarch, flour, and cold water, then mix well to make the flour batter.*

2) *Peel the bananas, and cut each banana into 5 diagonal pieces. Dip each banana piece into the flour batter to coat it. Deep fry the pieces in hot cooking oil for about 1 minute, or until they are golden. Remove the bananas and drain off the oil from wok.*

3) *Brush the serving plate with some sesame oil. This will add extra aroma and the babana fritters tend to not stick to the plate.*

4) *Heat 1 tablespoon of cooking oil in a wok, add sugar and water, stir fry over low heat until it turns into syrup. Turn off the heat, add the bananas, and mix carefully. Remove the bananas from the wok onto a plate to serve.*

Almond Float

Almond float is a refreshing dessert that can be served with canned or fresh fruit.

Serves: 4–6

Ingredients:

Unflavored gelatin	: 1 envelope	Evaporated milk	: 1 cup
Granulated sugar	: 4 tbsp	Cold water	: 1 cup
Boiling water	: 1 cup	Fruit cocktail	
Almond extract	: 2 tsp	with syrup	: about 500 gms

Procedure:

1) In a medium bowl, combine the gelatin and the sugar, stirring to mix well.

2) Pour the boiling water over the gelatin/sugar mixture, and stir until completely dissolved.

3) Stir in the almond extract, evaporated milk, and the cold water, blending thoroughly.

4) Pour the gelatin into a bowl or serving mold if desired. Chill until firm.

5) To serve, cut the gelatin into 1-inch squares or diamonds and serve with the canned fruit and the syrup from the can. The almond float may be prepared in advance and refrigerated (not frozen) until ready to serve.

Note:

• You can substitute lemon or vanilla extract in place of almond extract.